D0916008

Prophetic Faith
and the
Secular Age

Prophetic Faith
and the
Secular Age

Levi A. Olan

KTAV PUBLISHING HOUSE, INC., NEW YORK

INSTITUTE FOR JEWISH STUDIES, DALLAS
1982

Library of Congress Cataloging in Publication Data

Olan, Levi Arthur, 1903-
   Prophetic faith and the secular age.

   Includes bibliographical references.
   1. Prophets. 2. Theism. 3. Civilization, Modern—
20th century. I. Title.
BS1198.O38   200′.1   82-2903
ISBN 0-87068-888-X   AACR2

Manufactured in the United States of America

For Sarita

Contents

Preface

The manuscript for this volume was read by several scholars and friends who gently offered their criticisms and helpful suggestions. Sheldon Blank and Bernard Bamberger of the Hebrew Union College–Jewish Institute of Religion; James Ward and William Power of the Perkins School of Theology; Decherd Turner, former director of Bridwell Library; Jack Bemporad, Temple Emanu-El, Dallas, Texas; Sarita Olan, who translated an illegible scribbling into the final manuscript: Leo Fields, who materially made possible the publication of the volume. I am grateful to all of them. They are not responsible for the shortcomings this book certainly has.

Translation from the Hebrew Bible are from *The Torah* and *The Prophets*, Jewish Publication Society, 1962, 1978.

Introduction

The complexities of the crisis today seem to defy man's best efforts to resolve them. The constant threat of a nuclear holocaust, the total annihilation of human life by environmental pollution, and the rapid exhaustion of natural resources are beyond modern man's comprehension, and therefore beyond his ability to overcome them. It is not surprising that some people wonder whether the writings of the wise men of yesterday may be examined for some light upon the present dilemma. The riddle of human history, it is often suggested, is basically the same for all ages, and its resolution lies in man's recognition of the existence of a universal truth. Reinhold Niebuhr, in his *Introduction to Faith and History,* wrote: "This volume is written on the basis of faith that the gospel of Christ is the same yesterday, today, and forever."[1] In a similar vein, a modern Rabbi assures us that the cure for modern man's agony was prescribed by the Hebrew prophets who lived almost three thousand years ago. "To ignore them," he writes, "is to court death and destruction in any era. To accept their message and apply it individually, nationally, and internationally, is to embrace salvation and survival."[2]

The proposition that Isaiah, Plato, Buddha, and Jesus spoke truths relevant to our age and all ages is accepted by many modern people. However, a mind fashioned by twentieth-century science cannot view the universe as did those who lived in a three-storied universe populated with angels and demons. "We cannot see the world as the first century saw it," writes Van A. Harvey; "We have, as it were, bitten of the apple and our eyes are opened, and our memories are indelibly stamped with the new vision of reality. . . . Although we can transcend it (our new consciousness) from time to time in an act of historical imagination, we judge what we understand in the light of our present knowledge, and interpret it in terms of our own existing world."[3] In the present hour of worldwide confusion and helpless frustration, the accumulated wisdom of the past is worthy of serious consideration. We should be aware that it comes to us in words and symbols of an earlier age, and that it was directed to people who faced perplexing problems particular to their time, and it was expressed in cultural symbols native to them. It is important that we seek to understand their predicament in terms of the conditions in which they lived, being mindful of the fact that the culture in which they moved about differs.from ours. The resolutions by their wise men to the perplexities they faced will in some measure appear to us to be dated and inapplicable to our critical situation.

This book will concern itself with the faith of the Biblical prophets and its relevancy to the perplexities of the human condition today. The present feeling of frustration is haunted by the seers of old. "We are disturbed to discover," writes Harvey, "that we are wresting with the same old issues, that the same questions have returned again in only a slightly different guise. With that realization, the possibility suggests itself in the back of our minds that the answers once proposed may not be so fantastic as we had so smugly assumed. We find ourselves rethinking the thoughts of those whose conclusions we look upon with disdain. This is always painful."[4] Harvey in this passage is writing about the intellectual climate of the nineteenth century. It is, however, equally valid for the prophetic message spoken three millennia ago. Somehow Amos, Isaiah and Jeremiah stalk the present.

Biblical literalists point to chapter and verse which had predicted the latest current event. This represents a total misunderstanding as well as an unwarranted misuse of the prophetic message. The Hebrew prophets were not soothsayers; some of their predictions about particular events never took place. The Medes did not destroy Babylon as Jeremiah had predicted,[5] and Cyrus never became a worshipper of Yahwe as Deutero-Isaiah had foretold.[6] The validity of the prophet's message did not depend upon the fulfillment of his prediction of a particular event at a given time and place. He was confident of two basic truths of human history—God as judge of men and nations will bring judgment upon backsliding peoples, and his divine purpose will be realized in the end of days. Men may disobey God's will, but they cannot defeat God. The prophet possessed a profound insight into the process of human history. His view of contemporary events was fashioned by a God-faith unique in his time. He shared with the creative artist a rare gift of sensitivity to the profound meaning of those events. He saw and he heard that which escaped the eyes and ears of other men.

Nineteenth-century political radicals acclaimed the Biblical prophets as social reformers who paved the way for socialism. They are just as mistaken as the Biblical literalists who discovered an ancient verse which foretold the Johnstown flood. The prophetic writings do not contain a blueprint for the ideal political or economic social order, nor do they predict the next natural disaster. Their significance today is their assertion that men and nations are subject to universal moral laws which are an integral part of creation. The words spoken by the Biblical prophets are, probably, better understood today than they were by those who actually heard them. H. H. Rowley reminds us that "Hearing, they heard not, and even those who uttered the words can have perceived less their implications than we should. The Magna Carta should have a fuller meaning to us, who look back a thousand years of the unfolding freedom to which it led, than it could have had to those who framed it. And so the work of Moses, Elijah, and Paul lay not alone in what it was in itself, but in what it has continued in ages far beyond their horizons."[7] The theological frame in which the prophetic doctrine is disclosed tends to disconcert the mind of modern secular man. The idea of God omnipotent and judge of history is alien to the culture in which he lives. Meaningful to an earlier generation, it is meaningless in an age pervaded by science and reason.

Nevertheless, we are haunted by a suspicion that the problems to which the seers of old addressed themselves are essentially similar to those which perplex and threaten modern man. They spoke of poverty, inhumanity, cruelty, hypocrisy, injustice, and war; and are not these the very issues that dominate our troubled world today? We cannot help but wonder, somewhat skeptically, whether the principles by which the ancient prophets examined the critical issues of their day are applicable in part, if not in whole, to the human condition today. Their words seem to be speaking to us who are being assailed by prophecies of doom as conditions grow more cataclysmic and catastrophic. Modern culture is predominantly secularistic and is alienated by the theism which is basic to prophetic teaching. A report of a recent transdisciplinary convocation relates that at the conclusion of a paper read by a theologian, a physicist responded: "The speaker was quite intelligible until he introduced the word *God* in his talk. This word does not stand for anything within my range of concepts and experience; so every sentence was meaningless to me, and the whole paper was unintelligible. Will the speaker please tell us what the word *God* signifies." Modern man, like the physicist, accepts the use of words like *justice, love,* and *peace* even though he may not comprehend their profound meaning, but *God* is an incomprehensible word in his working vocabulary.

This book will examine the prophetic faith as it moved from the original Biblical through the Post-Biblical and modern periods of history. It will finally apply the neoclassical theology to it and try to determine its validity in the post-modern view of the universe which the new scientific revolution has revealed. The final chapter will describe the life and death crisis of the human condition today and ask whether this faith offers modern man realistic hope for benign resolution.

Chapter 1

The Creative Artist and the Prophet of God

The closest analogue to the Hebrew prophet is the artist. They are not to be equated, since the difference between them is critically important. What they share in common, however, can guide us in our understanding of biblical prophecy. The many paintings and sculptures of the prophets which the artists have made suggest a natural affinity between them. Psychologists sometimes place the source of the creative work of the artist and the prophet in the subconscious. They describe the prophet as one who responds to the unconscious needs which arise out of his personal conflicts and repressions. The artist, they say, is one whose "artistic creativeness is an expression of the unconscious in which compensation and sublimation play this prominent role. Thus warmth and color in Matisse, or the line of a theme of Mozart are to be elucidated as originated in the artist's unconscious but assuming the conscious form of wish fulfillment, defense mechanism, striving for recognition, or some other psychological effect."[1]

Everybody has a subconscious which takes some part in thought and action. The submerged guilts, conflicts, and repressions that all of us experience sometimes find relief in creative work. Ben Shahn, while acknowledging the role of the subconscious in artistic creation, nevertheless protests: "The subconscious cannot create art. . . . To the psychologist it is the periodic insanity of Van Gogh that is pre-eminent, and the psychologist deduces much from that. But to the artist it is clear that it was the great love of things and people,

1

and the incredible suffering of Van Gogh that made his art possible, and his insanity inevitable."[2] We must look elsewhere than the subconscious for the source of artistic creativity. Freud concluded that "[analysis] can do nothing toward elucidating the nature of the artistic gift, nor can it explain the means by which the artist works—artistic technique."[3] Hazelton suggests that both artist and prophet struggle and suffer, and endowed with a "heightened sensitivity, these induce clearer vision and result in the creation of new forms of meaning."[4]

Moses ibn Ezra, a thirteenth-century Hebrew poet, wrote, "A poet is called in Hebrew a prophet."[5] He is not suggesting that every poet is a prophet, nor that poetry and prophecy are co-equal. He is referring to instances in the Bible where a singer of songs is called a prophet. Thus, after the miraculous crossing of the Red Sea, "then Miriam the prophetess, Aaron's sister, took a timbrel in her hand, and all the women went out after her in dance with timbrels. And Miriam chanted for them, 'Sing to the Lord, for he has triumphed gloriously; Horse and driver he has hurled into the sea.' "[6] In one of the furious battles against the Canaanites we read that "Deborah, wife of Lapidoth, was a prophetess; she led Israel at that time." Following the victory, "On that day Deborah . . . sang."[7] David is described as "The anointed of the God of Jacob, the favorite of the songs of Israel," and spoke these last words, "The spirit of the Lord has spoken through me, his message is on my tongue; the God of Israel has spoken . . ."[8] Ezekiel complained that the people were looking upon him as an entertainer. "And I said: Ah, Lord God! They say of me: He is just a riddle-monger!"[9] God later confirms the prophet's protest; "To them you are just a singer of bawdy songs, who has a sweet voice and plays skillfully; they hear your words, but will not obey them. But when it comes—and come it will—they shall know that a prophet has been among them."[10] The Hebrew Scriptures correlate prophecy and song. Moses Buttenweiser, who was by profession a scholar and teacher of the Bible, was moved to write, "Psychologically speaking prophetic inspiration is not materially different from 'furor poeticus' of the master poet or artist."[11]

In Greek thought poets are possessed and inspired. Plato gave careful attention to the nature of the poet.

For all good poets, epic as well as lyric, compose their beautiful poems not by art, but because they are inspired and possessed. And as the Corybantian revellers when they dance are not in their right minds, so the lyric poets are not in their right mind when they are composing their beautiful strains; but when falling under the power of music and metre they are inspired and possessed. . . . For the poet is a light and winged and holy thing and there is no invention in him until he has been inspired and out of his senses, and the mind is no longer in him: when he has attained to this state, he is powerless and is unable to utter his oracles. . . . for not by art does the poet sing, but by power divine. . . . For in this way God would seem to indicate to us and not allow us to doubt that these beautiful poems are not human, or the work of man, but divine and the work of God; and that the poets are only the interpreters of the Gods by whom they are severally possessed. Was not this the lesson which the God intended to teach when by the mouth of the worst poets he sang the best of songs?[12]

In the *Apology* Socrates relates that in search of the meaning of the oracle

I went to the poets. . . . I took them some of the most elaborate passages in their own writings, and asked what was the meaning of them—thinking that they would teach me something. Will you believe me? I am almost ashamed to confess the truth, but I must say that there is hardly a person present who would not have talked better about their poetry than they did themselves. Then I knew that not by wisdom do poets write poetry but by a sort of genius and inspiration; they are like diviners or soothsayers who also say many fine things, but do not understand the meaning of them.[13]

In Plato's view, then, the poet creates not by his own wisdom or talent, but only when divine power possesses him. Shelley, centuries later, described poets as hierophants of an unapprehended inspiration.

Hesiod, a contemporary of the Hebrew prophet Amos, and like him a shepherd, relates his experience when he was grazing his flocks at the foot of Helicon, sacred mountain of the muses. He had been inspired by these goddesses with a mission unlike what any poet before him had ever received. "They breathed into me the divine gift of song that I should declare the things of the future and of former things."[14] Aristotle believed that there are two sources; "poetry demands a man with a special gift for it, or else, one with a touch of madness in him."[15] He speaks of the poet as one endowed with a "happy gift of nature" which lifts him out of his proper self. The mythology of ancient Greece assigned this gift to the Muses, the nine goddesses, who gave the poet his songs and sang them through his lips. The *Odyssey* begins, "Tell me, O Muse," and much later William Blake calls upon "Muses who inspire poet's songs." In a suggestive image the modern philosopher Croce wrote, "The true artist in fact finds himself big with his theme, he knows not how; he feels the moment of birth drawing near, but he cannot will it or not will it."[16]

Artists during the period of creativity are conscious that they are in touch with a source outside of themselves. Like Jeremiah, who spoke of the fire which raged in his breast and could not be extinguished, the artist reports that he is enthralled, enslaved, or that he is under the control of the power of his inspiration. Goethe, in a letter to Eckermann:

> All productivity of the highest kind, all important insights and inventions, all great thoughts which bear fruit and have consequences—all these are things beyond any man's control and subject to no earthly power. Man must simply look upon them as unexpected gifts from on high, as pure children of God which he must receive and venerate with gratitude and rejoicing. This kind of thing is akin to the daemonic, that superior force which does what it pleases with human beings, and to which they unwittingly abandon themselves, in the belief that they are acting on their own impulses. In such cases a man can often be regarded as an instrument of some higher government of the world, as a worthy and chosen vessel of divine inspiration.[17]

Friedrich Nietzsche, referring to his writing *Thus Spake Zarathrustra* said: "I never had a choice." He went on to say that with the slightest remnant of superstition left, he could hardly have rejected completely the idea that the artist is "the mere incarnation or mouthpiece, or medium of some mighty power." He applies the word "revelation" to those experiences in which one hears but does not seek; one takes but does not ask who is giving. Everything occurs quite without volition, "as if in eruption of freedom, independence, power, divinity."[18] Nietzsche's use of "some almighty power" for the force which enthralls him borders on biblical language. But, unlike the prophet, he does not know who it is that enslaves him.

Some poets speak of hearing voices, others feel that they write at someone's dictation. Amy Lowell, a poet with scientific training, employed a less picturesque vocabulary. She denied hearing voices, but did have the sense that words were being pronounced in a toneless form. She defined a poet as "a man of an extraordinary sensitive and active subconscious personality, fed by and feeding a non-resistant consciousness. . . . 'it came to me' is really the best description of the conscious arrival of a poem."[19] In answer to the question how poems are made, she wrote, "I don't know . . . I meet them when they touch consciousness and that is already a considerable distance along the road of evolution. . . . the poet is something like a radio aerial, he is capable of receiving messages on waves of some sort; but he is more than an aerial, for he possesses the capacity of transmitting the message into those patterns of words we call poems."[20]

The artist, the poet, the creative person generally, is not a lifeless vessel bearing some extraneous message. There are times when the source of his inspiration acts temperamentally, striking his work at a critical point and there is not another move he can make. At this point the conscious training of the artist takes over and fills in, guided, however, by the inspiration he has received. In this sense an artist is both born and made. "He must be born with a subconscious factory," wrote Amy Lowell, "always working for him or he never can be a poet at all, and he must have knowledge and talent enough to putty up his holes."[21] The artist, then, begins with inspiration, for without it he is no artist at all, but he must also have talent if he is to turn his inspiration into a creative work of art. Talent without inspiration, and inspiration without talent, cannot produce creative work in the arts and the sciences.

The notebooks of da Vinci and Wordsworth testify to the proposition that the creative artist must both experience inspiration and possess talent. Stephen Spender describes the creative process this way: "Inspiration is the beginning of a poem and it is also the final goal. It is the first idea which drips into a poet's mind, and it is the final idea which he at last achieves in words. In between this start and this winning post there is the hard race, the sweat and toil. Paul Valery speaks of the *une ligne donné* of a poem. One line is given to the poet by God or nature, the rest he has to discover for himself."[22]

There is impressive evidence supporting the idea that creative artists are conscious of a power beyond themselves directing their work; William Blake, discussing his poem *Milton*, said, "I have written this poem from immediate dictation, twelve, or sometimes twenty or thirty lines at a time without premeditation, and even against my will; the time it has taken in writing was rendered non-existent. I am the secretary, the authors all in eternity."[23] Ernest Jones, in *Hamlet and Oedipus*, relates that D'Annunzio, the Italian poet-dramatist, makes one of his characters "experience extraordinary movement in which his hand had written verse that had seemed to him not born of his brain, but dictated by an impetuous deity to which his unconscious organ had obeyed like a blind instrument."[24] Tchaikovsky spoke of a "supernatural and inexplicable force one calls inspiration."[25] Paul Klee, whose art often appears light and playful, wrote that everything vanishes around him, and good works rise of their own accord. "My hand is entirely *the implement* of a distant sphere. It is not my heart that functions but something else, something higher, something, somewhere remote."[26]

A modern theologian is certain that the experience of the artist is divinely inspired. He writes, "whether he [artist] believes in God or not is unimportant, the fact is that God believes in him for the despair and delight of making the word become flesh."[27] Most artists will demur, for when he speaks of a power that enthralls him as inexplicably higher, distant, or supernatural, the artist generally does not mean God. Rodin once said that artists are the most religious men. He did not mean what our theologian does. He was merely proposing that the artist has the sense of vocation which the prophet also has, the sense of being called. Both know that they are not working at an occupation or at a profession. It is true that the message which the prophet receives is from God—of that he is certain. The artist cannot identify who or what has called him.

A second quality shared by the prophet and the artist is their involvement in the human condition of their time. The biblical prophet heard God speak in the midst of a real historical situation. He observed the events of his day and saw in them what other men could not see. "And He said, 'Go, say to that people: Hear, indeed but do not understand: See, indeed, but do not grasp.' "[28] Moses, of whom Scripture says that there has not been a prophet since like unto him, hears God's call only after he had looked upon the cruel slavery which the Hebrews endured. He became so outraged by the scene of an Egyptian taskmaster viciously beating a slave that he slew the Egyptian. This experience, common at that time and in that place, prepared him to hear God call him from the midst of the burning bush.[29] The prophetic mission did not derive from quiet meditation or concentration, as in the case of the mystic. The prophet is called to proclaim God's word out of the agony of a specific human situation. The classic prophet had moved far beyond the soothsayer or diviner of an earlier period. He had what the French call an *engagement* with the world, caught up in it and involved in it. He was part of a program or a cause. He was aware that he was being called to do something.

The German poet Rilke said that a poet must experience deep dimensions of the human condition before he can write a single line.

Ah, but verses amount to so little when one writes them young. One ought to wait and gather sense and sweetness a whole life long, a long life if possible, and then, quite at the end, one might perhaps be able to write ten lines that were good. For verses are not, as people imagine, simply feelings (these one has early enough),—they are experiences.

For the sake of a single verse, one must see many cities, men, and things; one must know the animals, one must feel how the birds fly, and know the gesture with which the little flowers open in the morning. One must be able to think back to roads in unknown regions, to unexpected meetings and partings one had long seen coming; to days of childhood that are still unexplained, to parents

whom one had hurt when they brought one some joy and one did not
grasp (it was a joy for someone else); to childhood illnesses that so
strangely began with such a number of profound and grave transfor-
mations, to days in rooms withdrawn and quiet and to mornings by
the sea, and to the sea itself, to seas, to nights of travel that rushed
along on high and flew with all the stars—and it is not yet enough if
one may think of all of this. One must have memories of many nights of
love, none of which was like the others, of the screams of women in
labor, and of light, white sleeping women in childhood closing again.
But must also have been beside the dying, must have sat beside the
dead in the room with the open window and the fitful noises. And still
it is not yet enough to have memories. One must be able to forget
them when they are many and have the great patience to wait—until
they come again. For it is not yet the memories themselves. Not till
they have turned to blood within us, to glance and gesture, nameless
and no longer to be distinguished from ourselves—not till then can it
happen that in a most rare hour the first word of a verse arises in their
midst and goes forth from them.[30]

The artist, like the prophet, moves sensitively through the bright
lights and the dark shadows of life about him. It is in this experience
that he hears the call which impels him to the act of creation. Great
artists are usually found where life is at its most intense. "Genius is
inspired by life—talent by art. Genius shocks, talent smooths."[31]
Agony and pain brought forth Picasso's *Guernica* and Britten's *War
Requiem*, just as they called Amos to cry out "Thus said the Lord:
For three transgressions of Israel, for four, I will not revoke it [i.e.,
the decree of punishment]."[32] A portrait painted by Rembrandt,
whether of himself or an unnamed old man, tells us that the artist
has looked deep into the wretchedness of life and has also reveled in
its glory. "A painter mingles with the world," wrote Abraham Rattner, "then, when he finds himself in the pit—in the arena—the
spectator as well as the gladiator, before a frightening spectacle, at
once terrifying and magnificent, how can he help the manifestation
of his terror, wonder, anguish, ordered and impregnated by the
qualities of his sensibilities into color related to color, to light, to
line, and all of it directed toward some majestic form, a symphonic
structure, the metaphoric transfiguration of it all."[33] Rattner describes art as the work of an "honest, outspoken puncher" and

"straight from the shoulder art." The artist who really matters questions "Our time, our way of life, our human qualities . . . the low, so-called degraded, as well as the lofty . . . self-realization and self-sacrifice together."[34]

The artist and the prophet share an awareness of a reality which Rattner describes as "deeper than that which our eyes and our capacities to weigh and measure can grasp, the reality in back of the shadows."[35] The human scene they observe often disgusts both of them, and they use their talent to transmit their feelings to others. They have looked upon a world gone awry—Philip Roth's *Portnoy's Complaint* or Tennessee Williams's *Cat on a Hot Tin Roof*. The artist, like the prophet, parts the curtains to reveal the rotting foundation. The Theater of the Absurd of Beckett and Ionesco bears an affinity to Deutero-Isaiah's lament: "Why do you spend money for what is not bread, your earnings for what does not satisfy?"[36] The genuine artist and the true prophet are not entertainers; they do not paint pretty pictures, sing tuneful melodies, or proclaim pleasant visions. Their souls have known the wretchedness of life too painfully to gild it with bright colors.

The varying degrees of disenchantment and disgust which characterize much of modern artistic expression tells us that the artist has been to the mountaintop and seen a vision. He who has experienced the glory of life is driven to revulsion at the vile and corrupt which surrounds him. Like the priest, the artist has been inside the Holy of Holies and is smitten by the unclean and profane when he enters the city of men. The artist, more than most men, knows how far man has fallen below the vision of the good and the beautiful. Modern art reveals a somber and sober message alerting us to the glory of life we have discarded. Dissonance in music, disorder in painting, formlessness in sculpture, unmetrical poetry—these and similar characteristics of modern art are understood best as a protest against the vulgarization of the ideal. James Joyce carried with him a young man's memories of a beautiful Ireland, and the tradition of a Roman cathedral. His creative writing unveils the tender and the hallowed of his life experiences. Douglas Stewart called him an apocalyptic writer: "He rends the veil and looks beyond this world and this life to the dark void once lit by faith and hope. . . . He looks upon the void and dares to bring into conscious expression the fear which lies in the soul of the twentieth century, that the glory of man is meaningless."[37]

The modern poet-artist is today the dominant voice of moral grandeur and angry protest. He replaces the religious prophet, whose announcement "Thus saith the Lord" has been silenced. The priestly officiant at the altar of Church and Synagogue seems to be blind to the wretchedness of the human condition and deaf to the people's cry of despair. The artist has become, unintentionally, a moral alarm clock awakening us to the fallen state of human life today. "Art," said Paul Klee, "does not reproduce the visible, rather, it makes visible."[38] It exposes our illusions and tears asunder our complacencies. Pope Paul VI, at the official opening of a newly built chamber adjoining the Sistine Chapel, stood surrounded by the creative work of 250 modern artists. Among the artists represented in the exhibition were Picasso, Dali, Braque, Klee, Kandinsky, Lipschitz, Moore, and Baskin. The Pope said that these works of modern art represent an expression "beyond the genuinely human, also that which is religious, divine, and Christian."[39]

Some of these artists are not Christians, and most of them are not known for works on a religious theme in the traditional sense. They generally portray secular man in his day-to-day life in a secular world. Their works do not portray either the beautification or the glorification of the human condition. In the main they reveal the broken and twisted, the rough and the ragged. They report what they have seen behind the cosmetic curtain which conceals from our eyes the distasteful reality. They make visible that which escapes our jaded senses. They unhinge and unloosen us, they shock and arouse us. They summon us to "arise and shine," to crawl up and out from the gross darkness that covers the earth. The similarity in the roles of the artist and the prophet should not blind us to the critical difference between them. The spokesman for God called to men, pleading, sometimes threatening, that they turn from their evil ways and live. The artist, however, is not conscious of a message in his work, he is not a preacher summoning men to conversion. His special sensitivity and his genius impel him to reveal the grim reality of human existence. At best he permits a fleeting glimpse of the good and the beautiful. The creative artist is, unknowingly, engaged in the work of transfiguration.

The Bible distinguishes between true and false prophets. We shall pursue this theme more fully in the next chapter. Here we want to suggest that creative artists, like the biblical prophets, may be classified as true and false, and that the distinguishing character-istic is, in large measure, the same in both of them. The true prophet proclaims a message given to him by God which speaks to the human condition. He does not reveal the fruit of his own reflection, nor the outcropping of his unconscious. He is a true prophet only when his message is given to him by God. The truly creative artist does not feel called upon to portray pleasing fantasies or to create clever arrangements. He is called neither to please nor to dazzle. Beethoven and Rembrandt, Jackson Pollock and Jacob Epstein create only what the power of inspiration compels.

False prophets, the Bible says, are those who bewitch an audi-ence for a moment and then exploit it to lead the people to the worship of alien gods. The true prophet is at all times in the power of God, no matter how high the cost to himself. The prophetic message was not held back until the market was favorable. "A lion has roared, Who can but fear? My Lord God has spoken, Who can but proph-esy?"[40] Great artists often create upon a commission from a paying patron. Mozart and Michelangelo produced memorable works of art upon request, and sometimes on demand. Are they, then, false artists? Matisse rejected the suggestion that his work has a message; his art, he said, is intended to give pleasure. Can he be denied the role of a true artist? Listening to Mozart's music one would never know that there was oppression, servitude, and misery in Vienna in the eighteenth century. His music was written to satisfy the upper class and the aristocrats. Julius Portnoy suggests, however, that "The colorful canvases of Van Gogh and Matisse are an escape from the drab world that most of us know."[41]

Roger Ortmayer writes: "Instead of giving us an illustration, what the artist does is to celebrate. In celebration he arouses the clusters of associations and analogues that stimulate the poetic imagina-tion."[42] Art in post–World War II has moved beyond celebration. "It has re-asserted itself by demanding direct experience," says Ort-

mayer; "it has probed the edges of creativity itself. In all of this surge
of life there are dangers, mistakes, and frauds. But there is power
too—the kind of power that feeds into true religion."[43] The genuine
artist today, like the true prophet yesterday, is not vying for popular
applause. He creates at the risk of censure and condemnation. His
canvas of fragmentation and confusion reflects the brokenness of
human existence; his musical cacophony shouts aloud the noise of
emptiness which echoes the hollowness of man's life today; his work
is mocked, rejected, and scorned.

Why does the modern creative artist choose this unpopular and
materially unrewarding role? The simple answer is that he cannot
help himself, he is possessed, he is never for sale. The true artist,
like the true prophet, is ready to be damned, to represent his
inspiration in his art, indeed to represent it in abstract symbols. In
his essay on Baudelaire, T. S. Eliot proposes that "to be human a
man must do evil or good, and it is better, in a paradoxical way, to do
evil than to do nothing, at least we exist. It is true to say that his glory
is his capacity for damnation. The worst that can be said for most of
our malefactors, from statesmen to thieves, is that they are not men
enough to be damned."[44] The true artist, then, like the true prophet,
is man enough to risk damnation when a higher power calls.

Robert Frost artlessly confessed that he had a lover's quarrel with
the world. Every true prophet and true artist can make a similar
confession. It is out of a deep love for the world and for man that they
expose the layers of distortions that have smothered the good and
the true in those who have gone astray. The Hebrew prophets,
sometimes in anger, often in rage, had prophesied the captivity of
Israel by a foreign power, its slavery in the land of the captor, and
even its ultimate destruction. Such prophecies of doom they proclaimed upon their own people, in the name of God, because of their
people's rebellion against God's will. But it is the bitter anger of a
lover disappointed by the faithlessness of his beloved.

The prophet Hosea had known such disappointment when his
wife Gomer, whom he loved, strayed into harlotry and ended,
finally, forsaken and in slavery. His deep love for her moved him to
redeem her and bring her back home, where she had to live apart
from everyone, including her husband, until she was cleansed of the

shameful ugliness which had possessed her. In this painful personal experience the prophet recognized and understood God's relationship to his people Israel whom he loves, and had chosen and nurtured. Israel, like Gomer, went astray, whoring after strange gods and following their pagan way of life. In a moving passage Hosea describes God's love for Israel and his punishment for their faithlessness.

> I fell in love with Israel
> When she was still a child;
> And I have called [him] my son
> Ever since Egypt.
> Thus were they called,
> But they went their own way,
> They sacrifice to Baalim
> And offer to carved images.
> I have pampered Ephraim,
> Taking them in my arms;
> But they have ignored
> My healing care.
> I drew them with human ties
> With cords of love;
> But I seemed to them as one
> Who imposed a yoke on their jaws,
> Though I was offering them food.
> NO!
> They return to the land of Egypt.
> And Assyria is their king.
> Because they refuse to repent,
> A sword shall descend upon their towns
> And consume their limbs
> And devour [them] because of their designs.
> For my people persists
> In its defection from Me;
> When it is summoned upward,
> It does not rise at all.
> How can I give you up, O Ephraim?
> How surrender you, O Israel? . . .
> I have had a change of heart.
> All my tenderness is stirred.

I will not act on my wrath,
Will not turn to destroy Ephraim.
For I am God not man.
The Holy One in your midst:
I will not come in fury. [45]

This divine cry of pathos echoes the wisdom of Proverbs: "For whom
the Lord loves he corrects, even as a father the son in whom he
delights."[46] In contrast to the true prophet, the false prophet helped
the people hide from themselves their moral blemishes and their
spiritual harlotries. They beguiled them with messages of divine
favor and victory over their enemies. They cried "peace, peace"
when there was no peace. They were popularly applauded and well
rewarded by kings and priests. They loved themselves, they did not
love the people.

The work of many modern artists can readily lead us to view them
as angry men, disappointed and wrathful with the world. Their
disappointment and anger is not unlike that of the prophet, the
anger of a lover who suffers the pathos of one who cares passionately.
The artist today, more than anyone else, is keenly sensitive to the
disarray and degradation of the human condition. "From this immediacy in love the artist cannot tear himself loose. He is bound to the
world. Whether he deals with the world in forms that are harmonious or dissonant, forms that disclose an ideal or a bitter vision, the
bondage remains. And all of his efforts are ultimately a kind of
tender celebration."[47] The human condition today disturbs the spirit
of the artist. He loves mankind too much, and too passionately, to
whistle a sweet melody or to paint a pretty picture. His beloved lies
contorted, broken, and doomed; what can he be but a man of
sorrows, a man suffering the pathos of a lover!

"The despair of the artist is never total," writes Burger, "it excepts
his own work."[48] Normally we do not think of the poet or painter, the
novelist or musician, of the creative artist generally, as one engaged
in a didactic enterprise. He is the first one to reject such an interpretation of his work. Whatever truth does shine through his art is not
put there consciously. Picasso believed that "Art is a lie that makes
us realize the truth." The special gift of the artist lies in his ability to

transform the world of things and happenings, so that they confront us with the existent reality. "I don't have to distort," said Georges Braque, "I'm only making something out of nothing." G. B. Shaw, in typical Shavian style, laid down the dictum that "art should refine our sense of character and conduct, our self-knowledge, self-control, precision of action, and considerateness, and making us intolerant of baseness, cruelty, injustice, and intellectual superficiality and vulgarity."[49] Few artists, if any, will accept this description of their creative work. The genuine artist is guided by one basic principle, to report the truth as his spirit receives it. What men will do with the truth lies outside of his purview.

The prophet, on the other hand, is burdened with a conscious mission to transform the hearts of men, to persuade them to forsake their evil ways, and to enter a life faithful to the highest and the best as God requires. Like the modern artist they uncovered the broken and twisted reality of the world and of men. Their inflamed works often painted a terrifying picture of the holocaust that lies ahead. Thus Hosea prophesied, "Ephraim, too, must bring out his children to the slayers. Give them, O Lord—give them what? Give them a womb that miscarries, and shrivelled breasts."[50] This grim prophecy of doom led, however, to the prophet's didactic purpose: "Return, O Israel, to the Lord your God, for you have fallen because of your sin. . . . I will be to Israel like dew; he shall blossom like the lily, . . . He who is wise will consider these words, he who is prudent will take note of them. For the paths of the Lord are smooth; the righteous can walk on them, while sinners stumble on them."[51]

Wassily Kandinsky is one of the few modern artists who reflects verbally on the meaning of art. "Every work of art," he wrote, "is a child of its time; often it is the mother of our emotions. Only just now, awakening after years of materialism, our soul is infected with the despair born of unbelief, of lack of purpose, and aim."[52] Each period of culture, then, produces an art of its own which cannot be repeated.

A visit to a museum of modern art often baffles the viewer who is exposed to its exhibits for the first time. The art pieces seem to make no sense, arouse puzzlement, even scorn or mock humor. It all seems so hopelessly unintelligible. The mood of despair that followed upon the anarchy into which the modern world has fallen found expression in the novel, painting, sculpture, music, poetry, indeed in the entire creative works of the modern artist. They feel in their bones, as it were, that something terribly wrong has engulfed the life of modern man. They pick up soundings which no one else can hear, they see what the rest of us do not. Once again we have eyes that see not, ears that hear not. William Butler Yeats said it for all modern creative artists:

> Things fall apart; the center cannot hold;
> Mere anarchy is loosed upon the world,
> The blood dimmed tide is loosed, and everywhere
> The ceremony of innocence is drowned.[53]

In the first half of the nineteenth century Soren Kierkegaard, a Danish religious philosopher, picked up the soundings of the coming collapse of Western civilization. Reading his writings today, they reveal an author whose predictions of doom have, in large measure, been fulfilled. His sensitive spiritual antennae isolated the crucial flaw in modern culture. His prophecy was no more popular in his day than were the predictions of doom of the biblical prophets in their days. The tragedy of modern man, Kierkegaard argued, derives from his unqualified confidence in the utopian promises of the Enlightenment. In the passionate reliance upon reason and science, the foundation of the liberal hope, the Danish philosopher recognized the deadly germ which is infecting the body of human existence with a terminal disease. "It is intelligence," he wrote, "and intelligence alone that has to be opposed," and slyly added, "presumably that is why I, who had the job was armed with an intense intelligence."[54] Pure objectivity, he contended, is an impossible stance from which to examine what really matters in human existence. In this area truth is existential and must precede essence. The imminent advent of liberty, equality, and fraternity, which the French Revolution proclaimed, was destined to end in a tragic debacle. These liberal hopes were based upon an inadequate conception of the nature of man. Pascal in an earlier day had said, "The heart has its reasons, that reason knows nothing of." Hope based solely upon man's rational capacity is doomed to failure because, as Freud has taught us, men often unconsciously turn reason into rationalization.

Kierkegaard prophesied the collapse which began with World War I and has reached—after World War II, the Great Depression, Stalin, Hitler, and the Holocaust—a mood of almost total despair. An analysis of the social, political, and economic forces which brought on the present crisis is not integral to the major theme of this chapter. The proposal that a leap of faith is a satisfactory answer to modern man's basic problem is generally discounted. Our interest here is in Kierkegaard's prophecy, which lay dormant for almost a century. It is suggested that if he had written in German or French instead of Danish he could have received an earlier hearing in Europe. A more probable explanation for the delay in his recognition and his influence is that it had to wait until the disintegration of the human condition became evident and soberly challenged the confidence of the liberal faith. His writings were among the first, if not the first, which unmasked the false gods who were enthroned by the Enlightenment. The utopian premises of the goddess of reason and her attractive daughter, science, turned out to be a snare and delusion.

In the seventeenth century Spinoza had sounded the clarion call to salvation through reason. "Therefore, the more we endeavor to live under the guidance of reason, the less we endeavor to rely upon hope, and the more we deliver ourselves and make ourselves free of fear, and overcome fortune as far as possible, and finally direct our actions by the certain advice of reason."[55] Mankind, it appeared, was on the way—the ideal community of justice and brotherhood was as realizable as the water closet or the steam engine. The march of progress could not be stopped. Condorcet had listed the ten steps that lead from savagery to near human perfection. It is only a matter of time, and ignorance is the prime delaying factor. Education harnessed to science will translate man's dwelling place on earth into the prophetic vision of the City of God.

Despite the fulfillment of Kierkegaard's prophecy of doom, he cannot be classified among the biblical prophets. He made it very clear that he was not a prophet, or as he preferred to say, an apostle.

"I can lay no claim to an immediate relationship with God; I cannot and dare not say that it is He who immediately inserts the thoughts in me. My relationship is inwardness in reflection, the distinguishing trait of my individuality is reflection."[56] He disclaimed divine authority and never prefaced a prediction with the biblical, "Thus said God the Lord." He described himself as "an ordinary Christian" searching for the way that God and Christ will him to live. He even labeled as "pure bosh" the suggestion that he possessed a "genius for reflection." He acknowledged his reflective activity but distinguished it from genius. "For as far as one has genius, he has not reflection, and vice versa, in as much as reflection is precisely the negation of immediacy."[57]

He severely criticized Magister Adler's claim to a mission conveyed to him directly by Jesus Christ. Adler had announced that Jesus bade him to burn his earlier books and then dictated to him the greater part of a new book. Kierkegaard's closely reasoned treatise on this matter led him to a discussion of the larger theme of the relation of authority to revelation. When he disclaimed the role of prophet he said, "Mohammed protests with all his might against being called a poet and the Koran a poem. I protest with all my might against being looked upon as a prophet, and only desire to be a poet."[58] The critical difference between a genius and an apostle is the question of authority. The apostle Paul, who wrote some beautiful passages, as in I Corinthians 13, is not classified with either Plato or Shakespeare. His authority does not derive from the literary quality of his message or its aesthetic perfection. The genius, the man of supreme talent, is what he is by reason of himself; the apostle by reason of divine authority. The difference, Kierkegaard argues, is between immanence and transcendence. Modern man is uncertain about the reality of God. "Skepticism," he wrote, "has used this fact in order to put God on the same level as all those who have no authority, on the same level as the genius, poet, and the thinkers whose sayings are judged from a purely aesthetic or philosophic point of view; and then if the thing is well said, the man is a genius—and if it is unusually well said, then God said it."[59]

Kierkegaard insisted that the most gifted genius in art or philosophy cannot use his talent to receive divine revelation. He echoes the view of the biblical prophet: "For My plans are not your plans, nor are My ways your ways—declares the Lord. But as the heavens are high above the earth, so are My ways high above your ways, and My plans above your plans."[60] A fisherman or a shoemaker, a dresser of sycamore trees or a shepherd is as open to divine revelation as a poet or theologian, and probably more open. While Kierkegaard suggested the possibility of divine revelation occurring today, he argued that our age is so strongly committed to reflection and intelligence that it is well-nigh impossible. In biblical days a prophet became an immediate instrument. Today there is what he called a "serviceable factor" or "eminent reflection" which stands in the way of a divine call: ". . . he will think of himself and understand himself in the fact that this extraordinary thing has happened to him."[61] Kierkegaard manifested an element which is part of the prophetic office—he, before anyone else, heard the soundings of the coming destruction of Western civilization, and like the biblical prophets, he cried in a wilderness, unheard and reviled. Nevertheless, a thoughtful reading of his writings today leads to the suggestion that even though he was not a prophet in the biblical sense, he was, like the artist, sensitive to the wrong path that man has chosen. He was very much the poet.

The pie of progress became a slimy mess. Wars were fought with scientific weapons which threatened the annihilation of the human species. In a land renowned for philosophical and scientific excellence, men devoted their best brains to the erection of highly sophisticated gas chambers in which they efficiently asphyxiated six million men, women, and children. Leonard Hobhouse, a British liberal, spoke for the disillusioned: "It turned out to be, in sober truth, a different world from that which we knew, a world in which force had a greater part to play than we had allowed, a world in which the ultimate securities were gone, in which we seemed to see of a sudden through a thin crust of civilization the seething forces of barbaric lust for power and indifference to life."[62]

The mood of despair which followed the grand disillusionment settled first over Europe, where the collapse had come early and devastatingly. As with the fall of the Greek city-states, a failure of nerve had set in. Men began to lose faith in themselves as rational creatures and in the promises of science, which appeared to them more and more like the devil in disguise. Poets and philosophers dusted off the writings of Kierkegaard and discovered that the melancholy Dane of a century ago had been a true prophet. Western civilization, it seemed, had taken the wrong turn when it enthusiastically followed the signs which the Enlightenment had posted. Reason proved eminently useful and successful in weighing, measuring, manipulating, and controlling the world of nature. However, it proved hopelessly futile in answering the question of the meaning of human existence, or of salvation in its broad humanistic sense. Reinhold Niebuhr, as theologian and philosopher, declared that reason is a scandal. Logic and mathematics did not save men, they became a snare and a delusion. A new note was sounded, dark and somber, which announced that men had gone astray in their unquestioned confidence in the promises of the liberal utopia. The truth is, they were being told, that life is in its very nature absurd and hope lay either in Kierkegaard's leap of faith to God or Sartre's atheistic existentialism.

Fyodor Dostoevsky was a contemporary of the Danish philosopher. His novels explore the submerged and hidden spirits which lie deep in the human breast. His *Notes from the Underground* was published nine years after Kierkegaard. It is a story of a man wallowing in human depravity revealing the dark side of his inner life. The underground man represents all men who cannot rid themselves of their depravity by science, social reform, or by God. The hope which had rested comfortably on the Hegelian doctrine that the rational is real and the real is rational, and on the Newtonian order of nature, all of which led to Herbert Spencer's declaration that progress is inevitable—to this messianic vision Dostoevsky responded with a thunderous no. "Good Lord," he wrote, "what have I to do with laws of nature or with arithmetic, when all the time those laws, and the formula that twice two makes four, do not meet with my acceptance! Of course I am not going to beat my head against a wall if I have not the requisite strength to do so; yet I am not going to accept that wall merely because I have run up against it, and have no means to knock it down."[63]

The underground man solemnly declares that he often wished to become an insect but could never attain his desire. The yearning to escape being human is not unique with Dostoevsky. In his parable *Les Bêtes*, Pierre Gascar relates how the kingdom of beasts supplants that of men in the world of concentration camps and gas chambers. Kafka introduces a young man turned cockroach sitting with his family at the Sunday dinner table. James Thurber has pictured the waking of the animals behind the imperfect, rent covering of the human skin. "Since the *Letters from the Underground*," writes George Steiner, "we know that the insect is gaining on the part of man. Ancient mythologies dealt with men who were half-gods; post-Dostoevsky mythology depicts roaches who are half-men."[64]

The influence of Kierkegaard and Dostoevsky upon twentieth-century art and thought is amply discussed by critics and philosophers of our day. Germane to our theme of prophecy is the fact that both the Danish philosopher and the Russian novelist had prophesied the collapse of European culture a century before it began to happen. It is generally acknowledged that they were geniuses, yet they were more than men endowed with great talent. They were seers in the biblical sense, to the extent that they shared with the prophets and apostles a special gift of seeing and hearing that which nobody else could see or hear. They heard the soundings of the crisis that lay ahead for the Western world. Fear and trembling and the underground man have become the realities of our time. For them they were prophetic visions.

They shared with the biblical prophets several unique features. They were aware of and disturbed by the emptiness of the popular expressions of religious faith. Amos had blasted the people's confidence in the utopia which God will soon bring to them. "Ah, you wish for the day of the Lord! Why should you want the day of the Lord? It shall be darkness, and not light!"[65] Israel was living by the conventional religion of that day. They believed that if they satisfied the requirements of the Temple worship by bringing proper animal sacrifices to the altar, the "Day of the Lord" would surely come. For them it would be the great come-and-get-it day when God would save them from the threat of their powerful enemies and bless their lives with peace and plenty. The prophet, however, saw through such shallow faith. He knew by revelation that the Day of the Lord would be a day of judgment and of terrible darkness. In a similar vein Kierkegaard and Dostoevsky rent the veil which covered the established religious faith which beguiled the nineteenth century. Instead of the utopian modern version of the Day of the Lord that the Enlightenment was confidently predicting, they prophesied the advent of darkness and not of light, a time of dread and not of peace, a bitter defeat and not a glorious victory.

They also shared with the prophet a clear recognition of the irrelevance of the official institutions of religion common to their day. Jeremiah challenged worshippers hurrying into the Temple service,

> Thus said the Lord of Hosts, the God of Israel: Mend your ways and your actions, and I will let you dwell in this place. Don't put your trust in illusions and say, "The Temple of the Lord, The Temple of the Lord, The Temple of the Lord are these buildings." No, if you really mend your ways and your actions, if you execute justice between one man and another; if you do not oppress the stranger, the orphan, and the widow; if you do not shed the blood of the innocent in this place; if you do not follow other gods, to your own hurt—then only will I let you live in this place, in the land which I gave to your fathers for all time. See, you are relying on illusions that are of no avail. Will you steal, murder, and commit adultery and swear falsely, and sacrifice to Baal, and follow other gods whom you have not experienced, and then come and stand before Me in this House which bears My name and say: "We are safe" to do all these abhorrent things? Do you consider this House, which bears My name, to be a den of thieves? As for Me, I have been watching, declares the Lord.[66]

Jeremiah, like all the prophets, is not calling for an end to Temple worship. The attack was on the mistaken popular belief, encouraged by the priests, that ritual and sacrifice of animals at the altar are a substitute for justice and righteousness. "They were not rejecting ritual in its own sphere," writes Bernard Bamberger, "because they could not have imagined any other kind of cult. My own feeling is that in exasperation with the priesthood and the immoral society the prophets tolerated and never seriously pondered the question, 'If you abrogate the cult, what will you put in its place?' They hadn't heard Schechter's pointed remark 'you cannot live on oxygen alone.' "[67] Micah's oft-quoted statement which defined what God asks of man makes it clear that it is not burnt offerings. "He has told you, O man, what is good, and what the Lord requires of you: Only to do justice, and to love goodness, and to walk modestly with your God."[68]

Kierkegaard began his criticism of the church with an attack upon Bishop Mynster, who had confirmed him. This church dignitary, whom the state had appointed to the office of church president, was gifted with administrative skills, and with polished oratory brilliant enough to attract Denmark's leading citizens to an active role in church life. In all of this Kierkegaard saw Christianity's compromise with the state and with worldly interests. Instead of leading the people to stand before God and Christ, the clerics encouraged them to "listen with their hands folded over their stomachs, directing a sleepy look upward."[69] The church, symbolized by its bishop-president, became for Kierkegaard an enemy of Christ, who if he were to come again would be rejected by those who called upon him in the church. Dostoevsky transformed the bishop of Copenhagen into a demonic Grand Inquisitor who arrests Jesus when he returns to earth. The people kneel and worship Christ returned, but the "Cardinal knows better—tomorrow they will come to watch the doomed prisoner burn at the stake. Man wants neither God nor Christ, he wants the authority of the Church."[70] Alyosha's final judgment is that the Cardinal no longer represents faith, but is the spokesman for unbelief. For the Cardinal in Dostoevsky's story, "God had died, as Nietzsche was to proclaim a few years later."[71]

The creative artist and visionary philosopher also shared with the biblical prophet a common reaction by the community. The people misunderstood them and the authorities condemned them. Isaiah shocked the nation when he declared that Assyria would conquer Israel as the instrument of Israel's God, Yahweh. "Ha! Assyria, rod of My anger, in whose hand, as a staff, is My fury! I send him against an ungodly nation, I charge him against a people that provoke Me, to take its spoil and to seize its booty and make it a thing trampled like the mire of the streets."[72] It was a preposterous idea! Israel's God,

Yahweh, to whose altar they brought their choice animals as a sacrifice, will bring an idol-worshipping nation to conquer and to loot his own people. The authorities made short shrift of such demented troublemakers. They were imprisoned, thrown into pits, and driven out of the city. "Amaziah also said to Amos, 'Seer, off with you to the land of Judah! Earn your living there, and do your prophesying there. But don't ever prophesy again at Bethel; for it is a king's sanctuary and a royal palace.' "[73] The prophets confounded the people and unnerved their leaders.

The people of Copenhagen, some twenty-five hundred years later, were as shocked by Kierkegaard's writings as the Israelites were by the prophecies of Isaiah and Amos. They responded with hostile mockery to his criticism of the church and its clerical leaders. They shouted at him as he walked the streets, "Old man either/or" (the title of one of his books) and "The great philosopher with uneven pants legs" (one of his legs was shorter than the other). He spoke of himself as suffering the "martyrdom of radicals." His attack upon the church and its ecclesiastical leaders isolated him from everybody. He became a lonely and forsaken man, never arrested or imprisoned, although he expected it. "If a catastrophic effect is to be produced [his arrest, imprisonment, and possibly execution], what I had thought of doing was unexpectedly, after a period of complete silence, to utter 'the cry!' that the public divine worship is a mockery of God and to take part in it is criminal."[74] This Danish philosopher, whose prophecies influenced some of the great thinkers of the twentieth century, died in ridicule, forgotten by his countrymen and ignored by the church.

Among the twenty-one men condemned to be shot for revolutionary activities on the morning of December 22, 1849, was the author of *Notes from the Underground*. He was saved by an act of Czar Nicholas I, who "in his infinite mercy" commuted his sentence to four years imprisonment in Siberia. Dostoevsky was anathema to the Russian authorities, who charged him with treason because of his outspoken concern for the welfare of the common people. His sharp caricature of the church hierarchy brought upon his head the enmity of the theocratic State-Church of Russia. In his case, unlike that of Kierkegaard, when he died in 1881, he became a national hero. His novels became the pride of the Russian intellectuals. His experiences in Siberia form a large part of his writings. There he saw "strong men made sick" by the cruelty of the state and the indifference of the church. The peasants did not understand him, although he felt their sad plight in his bones. He let his cry of agony flow from his pen into some of the greatest novels in all of literature. In his case, too, it took a century for men to discover his prophetic insight into modern man's human condition.

These nineteenth-century writers have so much in common with the Hebrew prophets that the temptation to equate them is natural. They do show a heightened sensitivity to the deeper meanings of the events of their times, as well as the talent and the will to alert people to the dangers that lie ahead. They were profoundly religious men who unveiled the emptiness of the established religious order. They shared together the experience of being misunderstood by the people, and of bringing down upon their heads the condemnation of the political and religious authorities of their day. The most significant fact about them is that their prophecies were realized in history. The northern kingdom of Israel fell to Assyria as Isaiah had prophesied, and Judah was overrun by Babylonia as Jeremiah had predicted. The cataclysmic event which began in Sarajevo led to two world wars, the explosion at Hiroshima, and the present threat of nuclear annihilation. The script for this tragic drama was written by a Danish philosopher and a Russian novelist in the nineteenth century.

The prophetic voice is destined to fall upon deaf ears, whether it comes from the religious prophet or the secular artist. It is intriguing to speculate upon the difference it would have made to Israel if the people had attended seriously to Amos and Jeremiah. Would their life and destiny been less tragic? If the nineteenth century had thoughtfully considered the writings of the Danish philosopher and the Russian novelist, would much of modern man's catastrophic history been avoided? We will discuss in a later chapter the current prophecies of doom which are coming from the scientific laboratory, and ask ourselves whether we are thoughtfully listening. When the structure of Western civilization began to totter, some sensitive spirits of the twentieth century retrieved the prophetic warning

which had lain dormant for a hundred years. Karl Barth inaugurated
a school of thought described as "crisis theology." It directed attention to the critical sickness (crisis) from which modern culture is
suffering. The cause of this malaise lay in the anthropological,
immanentic, and optimistic view of the world which had been
fashioned by the Enlightenment liberalism of the nineteenth century. The Krisis for Barth and for his neo-orthodox disciples was
God's judgment upon a generation which placed its confidence
wholly in man's natural endeavors. In the nadir of despair the
thinking of these crisis theologians was featured in popular journals,
and the photographs of Barth, Tillich, and Niebuhr were on the
front cover of *Time* magazine.

Modern theologians were not the only ones who were greatly
influenced by the radical thought of Kierkegaard and Dostoevsky.
Secular philosophers also found the rational system of thought
described by Kant and Hegel, and the positivistic writings of
Comte, inadequate to explain the new human situation. The works
of Heidegger, Jaspers, and Marcel are concerned with *being* and
existence. Existential philosophy and theology initiated a radically
critical diagnosis of the sickness of modern man. Much of modern
art is existential in its protest against the neat and orderly view of the
human condition which dominated the Victorian era. The writings
of Sartre and Camus, the art of Picasso and Epstein, the music of
Schoenberg and Webern strikingly described the *Krisis* of modern
man. There is an eerie feeling that we have heard it all before. "Why
do you seek further beatings, that you continue to offend? Every
head is ailing, and every heart is sick. From head to foot no spot is
sound: all bruises and welts: and festering sores—not pressed out,
not bound up, not softened with oil."[75]

Existentialism penetrated the wall which the Enlightenment and
Emancipation had erected. The optimistic social programs for the
redemption of man which reason and science had engendered, and
which universal education enhanced, began to fall apart. Several
distinguished spokesmen for the social progress which liberalism
promised began to suggest that the mistake in their hopeful program
was their failure to take seriously the biblical view of the nature of
man. Daniel Bell, Harvard sociologist, confesses: "Modern culture,

particularly in its utopian versions, denies the Biblical idea of sin. Sin derives from the fact that man is a limited and finite creature who denies his finiteness and seeks to reach beyond it—beyond culture. Evil, as Reinhold Niebuhr has put it, does not exist in nature but in human history. . . . There is, therefore, progress in human history, but it is a progress of all human potencies, both for good and for evil."[76] These are certainly strange intellectual bedfellows: the Danish Christian philosopher, the American Paulinian theologian, and the liberal professor of sociology. The differences between them are far greater than the belated acknowledgment of the failure of liberalism to take seriously the biblical view of the nature of man. They illustrate the influence which the writings of Kierkegaard and Dostoevsky had upon our own generation either directly or indirectly. The prophetic nature of their works broke into luminous vision and helped fashion much of the thought and art of the twentieth century.

They were prophetic, but not prophets in the biblical sense. Kierkegaard, as we saw, drew a clear distinction between the genius and the prophet or apostle. The decisive difference is the factor of divine authority to which the biblical prophets laid claim. Their messages are to be believed not because they are reasonable and make good sense, although most of them can pass that test. They are true because the prophet received them directly from God. Kierkegaard disavowed any such role for himself and protested against all claims for such authority by others in his day, as in the case of Magister Adler. He argued that ours is an age in which intelligence and reflection predominate. Theoretically, he believed, it is possible for divine revelation to be received by a modern prophet. The cultural milieu, however, renders it almost impossible, because it would have to pass through a rigorous examination by logic, mathematics, and the natural and behavioral sciences. The declaration "Thus said the Lord" by anyone today is beyond comprehension.

Chapter 2

By Whose Authority?

A group of prophets arose in Israel during a period of three hundred years, from the eighth to the sixth century B.C.E. Some of their prophecies have been preserved and form a substantial part of the Hebrew Scriptures. They were preceded by earlier forms of *homines religiosi* both in Israel and other nations. The Zaku inscription and the Mari tablets tell of religious figures whose functions resemble those of the pre-classical Hebrew prophets. [1] In the biblical account of Saul's search for his father's lost asses we read: "Formerly in Israel, when a man went to inquire of God, he would say, 'Come let us go to the seer,' for the prophet was formerly called a seer." [2] Later Samuel tells Saul: "There, as you enter the town, you will encounter a band of prophets coming down from the shrine, preceded by lyres, timbrels, flutes, and harps, and they will be speaking in ecstasy. . . . he [Saul] saw a band of prophets coming toward him. Thereupon the spirit of God gripped him and he spoke in ecstasy among them. . . . When all who knew him previously saw him speaking in ecstasy together with the prophets, the people said to one another, 'What's happened to the son of Kish? Is Saul also among the prophets?' " [3] The Near East abounded in seers and prophets who performed not unlike the band of prophets whom Saul joined.

In Israel, however, there arose another type of pre-literary prophet who was primarily the spokesman for Yahweh, the God with whom Israel had made a covenant at Mount Sinai. His roots lay in

28

the social and religious experiences of Israel during its wanderings in the wilderness and in its conquest of the land of Canaan. The people were nomads whose style of life reflected the simplicity of shepherds. It was, as we might say today, a classless society, without a separation between rich and poor. Property, which consisted mainly of sheep and goats, depended upon finding a place to feed them. Leadership, both secular and religious, was vested in an elder. This nomadic period in Israel's early history was marked by blood kinship, with the family in the center. When Cain cynically asks: "Am I my brother's keeper?" he had removed himself from his kin, he was speaking as an outsider. The biblical twelve tribes of Israel considered themselves children of "Abraham our father" and blood brothers. The values by which such a community lives are sanctioned by the family and moderated by its elders, whose authority was generally respected. R. B. Y. Scott, discussing the nomadic era in Israel's history, writes: "Freedom of the desert and its untamed wandering life, together with a strong sense of clan brotherhood resulted in a strong and lasting love of liberty and equal justice."[4]

The settlement on the land transformed Israel from a nomadic to an agricultural community. The change radically affected the nature of its society and the values by which the people ordered their lives. A wealthy landowning class arose who set themselves apart from the serfs and slaves who labored for them. This new aristocracy required a different form of communal organization. A king who commanded a military force was needed to protect the property of the landowners from attack by foreigners as well as from marauders within. Tax collectors spread out over the land to extract increasing amounts from the poor to pay for the pomp and luxury of the royal house and its favorite vassals. The simple religious life which served a nomadic community gave way to an elaborate institution presided over by priests who became an independent class, set apart by their garb and authority. Ornate altars and sanctuaries were built, and elaborate rituals were introduced. The simple community of a family of families with its sense of kinship was converted into one in which the rich were set apart from the poor. The God with whom they covenanted at Sinai as their shepherd now became the King of

Kings who was ministered to by a special court of priests who
required of the people the best of their harvests and flocks in order
to gain the favor of God. This change from the nomadic to an
agricultural way of life radically affected every aspect of Israel's life.

The new society brought with it a new moral climate. The familial
kinship which characterized Israel during its nomadic period gave
way to a society in which the relationships were between master and
servant, king and subject, priest and layman. The moral code was
dictated by the needs and desires of those who controlled the
economic, political, and religious life of the nation. Prosperity now
depended upon the fertility of the soil, and the former shepherds
began to question their faith in Yahweh, whom they knew and
worshipped during their nomadic years. Their neighbors on the
land were farmers who worshipped Baal, the deity who made the
soil fertile. The rites with which Baal was worshipped were more
elaborate and sensual than the simple worship which they had
offered as nomads to Yahweh. Their neighbors worshipped their
deity with riotous feasting, dancing, and even the practice of prosti-
tution. It was difficult to resist the appeal of such religious sensual-
ity, since this pleased the gods, who made the land fertile and
produced plentiful harvests. It was very tempting to discard the
simple morality of their nomadic days and to ignore the covenant
their fathers had made with Yahweh at Sinai.

The initial protest against the flagrant breach of faith, and the
corroding moral influence that followed, came from a group of
prophets who were the immediate predecessors of the pre-exilic
prophets. Samuel, the first one mentioned in the Bible, spoke in the
name of the Yahweh tradition. He is described as both judge and
prophet, indicating that he represented both the political and the
religious interests of the community. In response to the new voices
calling for the establishment of a kingship in Israel, Samuel spoke
the words which have become the classical statement against all
monarchy and totalitarian government.

> This will be the practice of the king who will rule over you: He will
> take your sons and appoint them as his charioteers and horsemen, and
> they will serve as outrunners for his chariots. He will appoint them as

his chiefs of thousands, and of fifties: or they will have to plow his fields, reap his harvest, and make his weapons and the equipment for his chariots. He will take your daughters as perfumers, cooks, and bakers. He will seize your choice fields, vineyards, and olive groves, and give them to his courtiers. He will take a tenth part of your grain and vintage and give it to his eunuchs and courtiers. He will take your male and female slaves, your choice young men, and your asses, and put them to work for him. He will take a tenth part of your flocks, and you shall become slaves. The day will come when you cry out because of the king whom you yourselves have chosen; and the Lord will not answer you on that day.[5]

Less than a century later, during the reign of King Solomon, Samuel's dire prophecy was fulfilled. The familial community with which Israel began, and in which freedom and brotherhood were natural, was replaced by an autocracy too often tyrannical and oppressive. Prophetic voices echoing Samuel's protest reminded the people of their covenant with Yahweh, rebuked the royal rulers for the moral deterioration, social and personal, which they engendered. The prophet Nathan pointed his finger at King David, condemning him for ruthlessly robbing one of his subjects of his wife so that he might add her to his harem.[6] Elijah accused King Ahab to his face of faithlessness to Yahweh and Israel's covenant. When Ahab in anger cried out: "Is that you, troubler of Israel?" he retorted: "It is not I who have brought trouble on Israel, but you and your father's house, by forsaking the commandments of the Lord and going after Baalim."[7] From the tenth to the eighth century B.C.E. there were prophets in Israel who vigorously protested against abandonment of the covenant made at Sinai, and who strongly condemned the ready acceptance of the moral values of their idol-worshipping neighbors. The intensity with which these prophets of Yahweh delivered their message is attested to by the life-style of the Rechabites, who took their words literally. They refused to build houses, till the soil, or drink wine, because these were symbols of the new culture which was enticing the people away from the commitment which their fathers had made at Sinai.[8]

The development from these earlier prophets to the classical prophets who succeeded them was the result of the historic changes which saw the rise and fall of the great empires. The pre-literary prophets functioned in a historical setting limited to local and regional nations: Amorites, Moabites, Philistines, etc. But God had now become the director of world history, whose major concern was the welfare of Israel, its possible destruction and possible restoration. The eighth century saw the fall of the northern kingdom, as the prophets had prophesied. In the sixth century Judah and Jerusalem were conquered by the Babylonians, as Jeremiah had predicted. Yahweh could no longer be confined to one small nation, Israel. In the opening chapters of the Book of Amos, the Lord now judges the moral failures of Damascus, Gaza, Tyre, Edom, Ammon, and Moab as well as those of Judah and Israel. Yahweh had become the Lord of the universe, the God who required of all nations obedience to his moral commandments. The classical prophets became spokesmen for ethical monotheism. Yet they never cut themselves off from the prophetic beginnings of Moses and the nomadic experience of their fathers. Some mantic practices of an earlier day lingered on, and ecstatic experiences took place. Isaiah's call came in a vision of God on a throne surrounded by angels. The difference between him and the band of prophets whom Saul encountered is very great.

The importance of the preliterary prophets to the development of prophecy in Israel lies in the fact that they were spokesmen for the Sinaitic covenant with Yahweh, which was being abandoned by leaders and people alike. The role of the *navi*, prophet, was to declare the word of Yahweh and plead for return to him, and to the covenant their fathers had made with him. They preserved their nomadic origins as well as the moral values which were integral to its way of life. Elijah patterned his life-style after the nomadic model, dressing himself as a shepherd, and returned to the desert, where he heard the still, small voice of Yahweh. They were independent men beholden neither to king nor to priest. Like Micaiah they spoke only what Yahweh had told them even though King Ahab had said of him, "I hate him; because he never prophesies anything good for me, but only misfortune." In answer to the plea that he speak as the other prophets had, favorable to the king, Micaiah answered, "I will speak only what the Lord tells me."[9] The writings of these prophets are not preserved, and it is doubtful that they were ever written down. The account of their activities is recorded in the historical books—Samuel and Kings.

The writings of the classical prophets have been preserved and made part of the Scriptures, but these represent only a partial collection of the prophecies which they spoke, since many were either lost or not recorded at all. Furthermore, the texts we now possess indicate that there were emendations and rearrangements by later editors. These critical aspects are important and are found in a growing body of literature about the prophets. But for our purpose here we may affirm some general views about these literary prophets. They did not consider themselves innovators bringing to Israel a message which was unrelated to the earlier period of its history. Their prophecies were rooted in the nomadic period of Israel's history. "There she shall respond as in the days of her youth, when she came up from the land of Egypt."[10] The dazzling accouterments of a new and complex civilization had distracted the people from the basic values indigenous to their simple origins. "For my people have done a twofold wrong: They have forsaken *Me*, the fount of living waters, and hewed them out cisterns, broken cisterns, which cannot even hold water."[11]

The prophet was endowed with two special gifts which enabled him to perceive better than anyone what was really happening to the nation. First, he recognized the moral confusion which followed the shift from the simple nomadic life to the new complex urban society in which they now lived. The people, and especially the leaders, were caught up in the allure of the sensuous life-style of their neighbors. The priests and the professional prophets were supportive of the radical change. Only the prophet, who was committed to the covenant which Israel made at Sinai, was painfully sensitive to the sickness which was consuming the spirit of the nation. Second, the prophet possessed the unique gift of hearing God speak. He was open to the divine word. He viewed the events of history through the eyes of God, and saw Israel heading for disaster. "My people is destroyed because of [your] disobedience!"[12]

Modern man, come of age in a world dominated by science, responds favorably, and often enthusiastically, to the condemnation of injustice and the vision of peace "in the end of days" which are quoted in the name of the Hebrew prophets. The style and rhythm of their ethical messages have become an integral part of our culture, so much so that when we heard Martin Luther King, Jr., deliver his famous address, "I have a dream," we imagined that we were listening to Isaiah. As men with a rare insight into the conditions of their troubled times, and as noble spirits with a passion for justice and peace, the Hebrew prophets appeal to the human sensitivity of many modern people. It is their claim to a special experience with God in which they received a divine message to be delivered to the people that modern secular man cannot accept. It is a phenomenon which eludes a mind scientifically oriented. The *testimonium internum, Spiritus Sancti* bearing witness to our spirits that we are children of God, is foreign to modern man's way of thinking. John Skinner writes: "This immediate consciousness of having the mind of God is the ultimate secret of true prophetic inspiration, which being incommunicable can neither be analyzed as an objective criterion of an alleged revelation. . . . He who has it knows it, though he who lacks it may be deceived into thinking he has it."[13] This is not an acceptable criterion for modern man as he struggles to understand and deal with the strange and dangerous world in which he lives.

It is futile for a theist to discuss with an atheist the question of what God requires of man, since the atheist denies the existence of God altogether. This is modern man's dilemma with respect to the relevance of the teachings of the Hebrew prophets to present-day problems. They begin and end with the affirmation of the reality of a living God. Their thinking is theocentric; they are constantly in God's presence and wholly absorbed by him. They claim to hear the words of God and to speak his words to the people. To extract from the prophet's message a program for social reform or enduring peace divorced from divine authority is an act of intolerable emasculation. The prophet's message begins with "Thus said the Lord;" he does not present the fruit of his own wisdom or his personal moral doctrine. There is, to be sure, wisdom, morality, and social justice in the prophetic writings, but they are divinely revealed. The secularism which dominates the culture of modern man rejects the prophetic claim to divine authority but readily accepts much of the prophetic message as a noble, rational, and secular idealism.

Before we consign the Hebrew prophets to a distinguished niche in antiquity, acknowledging the importance of their role in Israel's history and in the development of Western culture—but no more, we should carefully examine the nature of their vocation. Their designation as *neviim*, prophets, describes them as spokesmen for God, who called them to perform a special task, to make known to the people the divine will. Each one became aware of his role as prophet in a different experience. "Never again did there arise in Israel a prophet like Moses, whom the Lord singled out, face to face."[14] Isaiah heard God's call while he was experiencing a vision of God seated on a high and lofty throne: "Then I heard the voice of my Lord saying, 'Whom shall I send? Who will go for us?' And I said, 'Here am I; send me! And He said, 'Go say to that people.' "[15] Jeremiah is told by God that he was born to be a prophet: "The word of the Lord came to me: 'Before I created you in the womb, I selected you. Before you were born, I consecrated you; I appointed you a prophet concerning the nations.' "[16]

The personal encounter between the prophet and God, as described in the Bible, is central to the prophetic faith, but it is alien to the modern secular mind. Biblical literalists have no problem with it, they firmly believe that for God all things are possible. The more sophisticated religionist explains by ascribing to the prophet a supersensitive imagination. The cynic accuses the prophet of practicing a deceptive trick, prefacing his own message with the declaration "Thus said the Lord" because in those days it carried authority. Jeremiah is a favorite subject for psychological investigation. More than any other prophet he reveals intimate details of his personal life. Major G. W. Povah suggests that these disclose symptoms characteristic of a psychoneurotic. He finds striking resemblances between the brooding Biblical prophet and Shakespeare's melancholy Dane.[17] Hamlet cries: "The time is out of joint; O cursed spite, that ever I was born to set it right!"[18] Jeremiah's first response to God's call was: "Ah, Lord God! I don't know how to speak, for I am still a boy."[19] Both men suffer loneliness, they are unsociable, longing for friendship, and they are melancholy persons. The prophet laments: "I have not sat in the company of revelers and made merry! I have sat lonely because of your hand upon me, for you have filled me with gloom."[20] Hamlet soliloquizes: "To be, or not to be: that is the question."[21] The prophet curses the day he was born: "Woe is me, my mother, that you ever bore me—a man of conflict and strife in the land."[22] Both men seem to be caught up in the grip of strong psychological forces, which prevent Hamlet, in spite of himself, from carryng out what he must do, and drive Jeremiah, in spite of himself, to do what he is determined not to do. The prophet has left us an eloquent description of his dilemma:

> You enticed me, O Lord, and I was enticed,
> You overpowered me and You prevailed.
> I have become a constant laughing-stock,
> Everyone jeers at me.
> For every time I speak, I must cry out,
> Must shout, "Lawlessness and rapine!"
> For the word of the Lord causes me
> Constant disgrace and contempt.
> I thought, "I will not mention them,
> No more will I speak in His name"—
> But His word was like a raging fire in my heart,
> Shut up in my bones,
> I could not hold it in, I was helpless.[23]

Was Jeremiah a psychoneurotic, a masochist, or merely a propagandist? Major Povah suggests that if we examine the lives of the Hebrew prophets and the Danish prince, we find that their behavior is alike in its abnormality. There is, however, one very critical difference between them which is important to our understanding of prophecy. The Danish prince is not the master of himself; his unconscious paralyzes him so that he cannot carry out what his conscience tells him to do. He does not recognize the nature of the psychic apparatus which is the cause of his actions; he never faces it, and he never masters it. His mission is accomplished by accident when his mother is poisoned by the murderer of his father, which sets him free to avenge his father. Jeremiah, however, is compelled to carry out his mission by a force he does recognize, and of which he is very conscious. It is "the word of the Lord," which has made him "a reproach and a derision all the day." He is persecuted, cast off by friends, thrown into a pit, and put in stocks, yet he is not free to deny God's command. The essential difference between Hamlet and Jeremiah lies in the fact that one never knew the nature of the psychic forces which controlled his actions, the other was very much aware of the power that drove him to act. Behind Hamlet was Shakespeare, behind Jeremiah was God.

The critical issue is the motivation of the prophet. Psychologists substitute various psychic forces to replace Yahweh. Walter C. Klein presents, in a brief summary, several such attempts to explain biblical prophecy in psychological terms. The fallacy in these lies in the fact that the prophet was dealing not with an invention but with Israel, the reality into which he was born. "If we search for some personal goal of need or desire in the prophet, we don't find it. We cannot name the thing that corresponds to the target: ambition, pleasure, security, etc., appear ridiculous. Prophets pursued none of these things, not even eternal life."[24] The prophets are not career men earning a living by prophesying. "They are not like the purposive organisms of psychology and vitalistic biology," Klein continues, "they constantly act against their own interests . . . and from the most eminent of them, Amos, Hosea, Isaiah, Jeremiah, and Ezekiel—the most radical surrender of the natural self is exacted. The prophet is inexplicable if his primary motive is self-development or even self-preservation. Hormic psychology helps to understand him, but does not lead us to the secret."[25]

Furthermore, the proposal that these men of ancient days, who left us some incomplete writings, are fit subjects for modern psychological analyses is not valid. "We cannot put Ezekiel under observation, we cannot interview Jeremiah, give an intelligence test to Micah, or a Rorschach to Joel."[26] The cultural gap which stretches between them and us cannot be bridged; the techniques of experimental and clinical psychology cannot be applied to the fragments of biography we now possess. Neither the prophets nor the collectors of their writings were preparing material for the twentieth-century psychologist. The biblical prophets are not to be understood by the erudite jargon of modern psychology. They were normal men with the "magnified normality that is the property of genius and sanctity." Freud concluded that "analysis can do nothing toward elucidating the nature of artistic gift, nor can it explain the means by which the artist works artistic technique."[27] In the previous chapter we discussed the relationship between the prophet and the creative artist.

Was the prophet a mystic? His personal experience with God does bear a resemblance to the *unio mystica*. But the prophet was not a mystic, since God reveals to him not himself, but his word. The prophet did not appeal to some special faculty in men by which they may instantaneously experience God. He does not even claim that for himself. There is no *Seelingrund* in the prophet which enables him to experience God. It is as creator of nature, and more particularly in the events of human history, that God reveals himself. The prophet was a sensitive observer endowed with a unique gift of recognizing God's role in both nature and in the events of human history. As a watchman of Israel he saw coming events long before anyone else—king, priest, or people. He was the guardian of the tradition of his fathers, to whom God had revealed himself in the act of liberation from Egypt. The prophet did not know God in a mystical experience or through subjective introspection. He heard the word of God and announced God's will to the people.

The mind of modern man, nurtured by science, is not at home with the experience of the Biblical prophet. His secular culture has no room for the existence of a God who spoke to the prophet the words he declared to the people. The prophet's declaration "Thus said the Lord" is a claim that he is the vessel through whom God conveys his message to Israel. He was chosen for his role by God, he did not choose it himself. He responded and surrendered to the divine call, but not always willingly. There was no school giving courses in prophecy which qualified a man to practice the trade or profession of prophet. There were disciples who attached themselves to a prophet and followed him about as he moved among the people declaring the word of the Lord. All of this, however, is alien to modern man come of age, who cannot comprehend so unworldly a phenomenon.

The prophets denigrated the "wise men" who brought to the troubled scene the distillation of common sense and the popular wisdom of the people. The wise men experienced the same social, moral, and religious conditions of their time, said the prophet, but they are blind to what is really happening to the nation. "Hear, indeed, but do not understand; see indeed, but do not grasp."[28] The prophet saw these same conditions through the eyes of God, who will bring judgment upon Israel and cause it to suffer for its wanton disregard of its covenantal responsibilities. "I will turn Jerusalem into rubble, into dens for jackals; and I will make the towns of Judah a desolation without inhabitants. What man is so wise that he understands this?"[29]

The prophet stood in a unique relationship to the present and the future which gave wisdom to his prophecy. "The message of the prophet," writes Scott,

> was differently related to the temporal setting of life. Time has two aspects; it goes on passing in ceaseless movement; the generations rise and pass away. But some present moments stand out from others. The hour strikes; the moment of decision and supreme experience comes. In that moment there is more than an instantaneous glimpse of one drop of time as time's stream passes over the brink of the waterfall. It can be a *great* moment charged with eternal issues determining destiny. There and then the eternal stands revealed, claiming and challenging. The prophet, not the priest or the teacher, is the voice of God in that moment. He is the spokesman who can articulate the meaning of the eternal order and a divine reality. He discloses the moral crisis in which man stands unheeding. He declares which is the way of death.[30]

The claim of the biblical prophet to divine revelation as the source of his message eludes a modern mind conditioned by an empirical-rational mode of thought. Nevertheless, modern secular man cannot but marvel at the profound insight into the human condition of his day which the prophet's writings disclose. He saw it through the eyes of faith in Israel's God and in God's plan for Israel and all nations. There is no mythology in prophetic literature, and there is no systematic philosophy in it. What is there is what William Albright described: "Through simple fusion of implicit faith in the power of Yahwe with consistent realism in judging human nature, the prophet developed a devastatingly, empirical logic."[31] This was not, however, a system of thought carefully written in a textbook or dispassionately taught in a classroom to students of philosophy.

The prophet was a man with a divine message who was chosen by God to declare his word in the hearing of the people. He was not in the service of the state or of the Temple. He blurted out his prophecy whenever and wherever the spirit of God directed him. What he said at such times bore an urgency which called upon his hearers to decide and to act in that moment. He must speak whether anyone listened or not, "for the sons are brazen of face and stubborn of heart. I send you to them, and you shall say to them: 'Thus said the Lord God'—whether they listen or not, for they are a rebellious breed—that they may know that there was a prophet among them."[32] The prophet comes as a watchman sent to warn the people that for their wickedness they shall surely die. If the prophet does not warn the people, and the wicked man dies in his iniquity, "I will require a reckoning for his blood from you."[33] This awesome responsibility which the prophet must bear and which he fulfills is incomprehensible in terms of modern culture.

The validity of the prophet's claim that the word he speaks was revealed to him by God is open to question, since each prophet stamped his own personality on the divine message. God's word comes through differently both in style and in form as each spokesman proclaims it. While wholly under divine constraint, the prophet remained a free man confident in his vocation. "Indeed, my Lord God does nothing without having revealed his purpose to his servants the prophets."[34] He never considered himself a messenger boy, even though he was always under a divine commission. Each prophet is a unique person, distinctive in character and life-style. The divine message passed through him as light passes through a colored glass. It comes out colored by the mood, experience, and outlook of the particular prophet. The remarkable thing about his office is the balance he achieved between divine constraint and personal freedom.

It has been suggested that each message which the prophet delivered was not a separate revelatory experience; rather, that he was privy to the divine purpose and declared it as the occasion arose. "Having stood within the heavenly council," writes Scott, "the prophet knows what God has done and is about to do."[35] This substitutes the knowledge of God's past and future actions in place of the divine constraint, and supposedly gives him greater freedom to interpret God's will. There is little gained, however, to answer modern man's question by substituting a divine council for divine restraint. It is interesting only because it points to the basic problem which the twentieth-century mind has with the prophet's claim to have access to God's word. A. C. Ackerman carries this to its logical conclusion. Commenting upon the Biblical account of Elijah hearing the still small voice, he writes that it was "clearly the result of original meditation. . . . The manner in which Jeremiah expresses his inspiration is illustrative of the general prophetic habit to sublimate the facts of their inspiration. This deliberate subtilization of inspirational power . . . tends to cover up the commonplace nature of inspiration, or at any rate, to conceal the prophet's own psychological ignorance of the source of his prophetic calling."[36] This view probably reflects the modern temper toward the idea of divine revelation. A formula which can hold together the prophet's access to God's word and his own freedom as a person eludes the empirical-rational mind of modern man.

The problem becomes more complicated when the prophet demurs to bring God's word to the people because he personally is fearful of the consequences. When the message was a doomsday judgment upon the nation, he sometimes tried to divert God from his intention. When God showed Amos the plague of locusts which would devour the herbage of the land, Amos said, "O Lord, pray forgive. How will Jacob survive? He is so small." And the Lord relented, saying, "It shall not come to pass."[37] The role of the prophet was far from that of a mechanical instrument through whom the divine words passed impersonally and unexamined. He belonged to his people with all his being, pleading with God to show mercy even when the judgment is deserved. Israel's vision of Assyria dragging Israel into captivity brought from him: "That is why I say, 'Let me be, I will weep bitterly; press not to comfort me for the ruin of my poor people.'"[38]

Jeremiah has left us the very moving intercessary prayer he uttered when God revealed to him the terrible droughts which would come upon Israel. "Though our iniquities testify against us, act, O Lord, for the sake of Your name; though our rebellions are many, and we have sinned against You. O Hope of Israel, its deliverer in time of trouble, why are You like a stranger in the land, like a traveler who stops only for the night? . . . The Lord said to me, 'Even if Moses and Samuel were to intercede with Me, I would not be won over to that people.'"[39]

God was not moved by Jeremiah's fervent prayer for divine mercy as he was in response to Amos's plea. This dramatic encounter between the prophet and God raises serious questions for the modern reader of the Bible. God's rejection of the prophet's plea for mercy and his immovable determination to carry out his judgment of doom presents a stumbling-block to religious faith today. This will be discussed in a later chapter. Our concern here is the dilemma of the prophet who is constrained by God to speak his prophecy of doom to the people whom he loves and begs for them divine mercy and forgiveness. What is a modern mind to do with this?

One aspect of the prophet's experience borders on the magical. In ancient Egypt and Mesopotamia words uttered by a magician in an incantation, blessing, curse, or oath were more than symbols of ideas. Once spoken the word became operative, it did something, it took on materiality. The magician pronounced secret words which made something happen. The word itself was magic; once it was uttered, it acted. The Bible records instances where the word is more than an articulate sound conveying an idea. It becomes a substantive reality once it is spoken, it cannot be recalled before it acts. A blessing once pronounced is more than an expression of good will. Esau learned that to his sorrow when his twin brother Jacob, with the connivance of Rachel, their mother, stole the blessing from their father, Isaac. Even though the blessing was extracted by guile and trickery, once spoken it could not be retracted.[40] One of the most tragic accounts in the Bible is Jephthah's vow to sacrifice whatsoever came through the door of his house when he returned victorious from battle, to offer it up as a burnt offering unto the Lord. To his horror the first to come through that door when he returned victorious from battle was his only child. "On seeing her, he rent his clothes and said, 'Alas, daughter! You have brought me low, you have become my trouble! For I have uttered a vow to the Lord and I cannot retract.' 'Father,' she said, 'You have uttered a vow to the Lord; do to me as you have vowed, seeing the Lord had vindicated you against your enemies, the Ammonites.'. . . And he did to her as he had vowed."[41] In these instances, as in others in the Bible, words once spoken became independent of the speaker and cannot be recalled; they must perform their assigned task.

The prophets used the term *D'var Yahweh*, "the word of the Lord," as a technical expression for a medium of revelation. When God sends forth his word it "runs very swiftly."[42] "My word is like a fire—declares the Lord—and like a hammer that shatters rock."[43] "But the warnings and the decrees with which I charged My servants the prophets overtook your fathers—did they not?"[44] Isaiah expressed the power of the word poetically: "For as the rain or snow drops from heaven and returns not there, but soaks the earth and makes it bring forth vegetation, yielding seed for sowing and bread for eating, so is the word that issues from My mouth: It does not come back to me unfulfilled, but performs what I purpose, achieves what I sent it to do."[45] In the Biblical account of creation God creates everything, except the heavens, the earth, and man, by speaking the words "Let there be . . ." and there was.[46] The psalmist as a poet understood the power of the word: "By the word of the Lord were the heavens made: And all the host of them by the breath of his mouth. . . . For He spoke and it was; He commanded and it stood."[47] The divine word is sometimes personified: "Thy all-powerful word leaped from the heaven, and from the royal throne, into the midst of the land that was doomed, a stern warrior carrying the sharp word of thy authentic command, and stood and filled all things with death, and touched heaven while standing on earth."[48] The words which the prophet spoke in God's name were charged with vital power. "The Lord put out his hand and touched my mouth, and the Lord said to me, 'Here will I put My words in your mouth. See, I appoint you this day, over nations and kingdoms; to uproot and to pull down, to destroy and to overthrow, to build and to plant.' "[49]

When the prophet announces coming events it is more than a prediction; his words in themselves are active, the events he fore-told happen. He speaks God's word, whether it presages doom or restoration, and the *word* itself is the real force which brings it about. The word which issues from the mouth of the prophet is, George Foot Moore said, "a concrete reality, a veritable cause."[50] Amos was driven from Bethel because Amaziah the priest sent this message to King Jeraboam of Israel: "Amos is conspiring against you within the house of Israel. The country cannot endure *d'vorov* [his *words*]."[51] The magiclike nature of the prophet's word is another stumbling-block for modern man as he tries to understand its rele-vance to the world today. The supernatural character of the word of the Lord lies outside the realm of modern culture. The classical prophets had discarded the practice of ecstasy and frenzy which characterized the earlier soothsayers and diviners. They did claim to hear God speak words which possessed supernatural powers. The substance of what they spoke in God's name appeals to the modern mind as both intelligible and profoundly moral. They call for justice, mercy, humility, and love. "It is a great cosmic force," wrote Moore, "going out from the deity and operating in the world to create and sustain values which man at his best seeks."[52] Extracted from the theological shell in which the prophetic message is embedded, the words are certainly meaningful, inspiring, and relevant to the hu-man condition today. Yet, shorn of their divine source, the words of the prophet lose their distinctive and unique character, for he is a spokesman for God, he is not a secular humanist teaching ethics.

The letters with which words are formed have mystified men from the beginning. The ancients ascribed their origin to the gods. The American artist Ben Shahn had a passion for letters and words. He wrote an autobiographical essay on his lifelong love affair with them, and included some of his now-famous paintings to illustrate his theme. Recalling a Jewish mystic of the Middle Ages who had discoursed on letters and words, he writes: "So wrote the great mystic Abulafia who believed that in letters were to be found the deepest mysteries, that in the contemplation of their shapes the devout might ascend through ever purer, more abstract levels of experience to achieve at last the ultimate ineffable abstraction of union with his God."[33] Shahn also translated into a painting he called *The Alphabet of Creation* a legend from the *Seder Ha Zohar*, the Book of Splendor, a cabalistic writing of the Middle Ages. The legend says: "Twenty-six generations before the creation of the world twenty-two letters of the alphabet descended from the crown of God whereon they were engraved with a pen of flaming fire. They gathered round about God, and one after another spoke entreating each one, that the world be created through him."[34] For the creative artist a word may possess the quality of reality and have a life of its own. His sensitive imagination enables him to comprehend the *D'var Yahweh*, the word of the Lord, which the prophet had pronounced.

The Bible draws a clear distinction between the sacred and the profane, *L'havdil bayn kodosh l'hol*.[35] The ark of the Lord was *kodosh*, "holy"; human hands dare not touch it. When David was moving the ark of God to Jerusalem, at one point "Uzzah reached out for the ark of God and grasped it, for the oxen had stumbled. The Lord was incensed at Uzzah. And God struck him down on the spot for his indiscretion, and he died there beside the ark of God."[36] It is not difficult to understand that in a culture where a physical object, the ark of God, was holy and untouchable, the word of the Lord as the prophet received and declared it was a holy word. "He made my mouth like a sharpened blade, he hid me in the shadow of his hand. And he made me like a polished arrow, he concealed me in his quiver."[37] The prophet was confident that he was speaking the word of the Lord, not his own.

The prophetic writings support the view that most of those who actually heard the prophet speak doubted his claim that "Thus said the Lord." His prophecies generally predicted doom for the nation, an idea which contradicted the popular view of God's relationship to Israel. His role, they believed, was to give the nation victory over its enemies and to prosper them all the time, so long as they worshipped him with sacrifices at the Temple altar. The prophetic pronouncement of destruction for the people with whom God had covenanted sounded like the ravings of a crazy man, whose claim that he was speaking God's word was arrogant nonsense. He had no way to authenticate his assertion, since he experienced no ecstasy and did not go into a trance. This is what the professional prophets did, but the man who prophesied doom in the name of Yahweh gave no sign, nor did he perform a miracle to validate his assertion of divine authority. That the people rejected him is understandable, since his message was wholly out of character with the God they knew. The prophet was constantly challenged to demonstrate to the satisfaction of his hearers that his own unquestioned confidence in his experience with God was real and genuine.

At times he seized upon an object near at hand and used it to clarify his message. Amos pointed to a basket of *qayiṣ*, "summer fruit," and playing phonetically, he related it to *qeṣ*, "end." "And the Lord said to me: 'The hour of doom [*qeṣ*] has come for my people Israel; I will not pardon them again.' "[58] Jeremiah sees *shaqed*, an "almond tree." "The Lord said to me: 'You have seen right, for I am watchful [*shaqed*] to bring my word to pass.' "[59] There are several such wordplays in the prophetic literature. In each instance the prophet claims that God has directed his attention to it in order to demonstrate his message. In themselves these objects bear no message. The prophet perceived in each one a divine inspiration and turned it into an opportunity to declare God's will.

Modern man has a natural explanation for these prophetic experiences. It is nothing more than an association of ideas; the object, the summer fruit or the almond tree, awakens in the prophet a relevant idea. That is not, however, what the prophet says happened to him. He claims that it was God who led him to the object and through it made clear the divine message. The substitution of psychology, the association of ideas, for faith in God is common to the secular culture, as was noted above. The trouble with this naturalistic explanation is that it denies the essential nature of the prophetic experience. The prophetic writings disclose intelligibility, realism, and moral purpose. The prophets certainly thought long and hard over what was happening in Israel. There were others who observed the same events, who thought seriously about them and offered their own explanations. The prophet, however, differs from all others in his claim to have heard the word of the Lord and spoken that word to the people. The attempt to secularize the prophetic experience contorts it into something which violates the original. Professor Brichto makes a strong case for the proposition that in the Bible faith preceded revelation. "Either God exists, or he does not. Either God speaks to man, or he does not. Scripture says he does— that is to say, he did communicate on specific occasions to men of faith with such wondrous results as to crown those occasions with the name of revelation."[60]

The authenticity of the prophet's claim to divine authority was challenged by men who also proclaimed "Thus said the Lord" but delivered a message entirely different, and generally opposed to that of the classical prophet. Jeremiah announced the imminent defeat of Judah by Nebuchadnezzar to the same audience which had just heard Hananiah tell them, "Thus said the Lord of Hosts, the God of Israel. I hereby break the yoke of the king of Babylon."[61] It is evident that one of them is either deceived or is lying. Micaiah's prophecy that Israel would lose the battle against Aram was opposed by four hundred professional prophets who assured the kings that they would win. In this case there is the intriguing account of God putting a lying spirit in the mouth of these prophets to entice them to go to battle, "for the Lord has decreed disaster upon you," said Micaiah.[62] The classical prophets strongly denounced those who professed to be prophets of Yahweh when in fact they were false voices deceiving the people. Isaiah denounces both priest and prophet who "are also muddled by wine and dazed by liquor; they are confused by wine, they are dazed by liquor; they are muddled in their visions, they stumble in judgment."[63] Micah accuses the priests of teaching for hire and the prophets of divining for money, "Yet they rely upon the Lord, saying, 'The Lord is in our midst; no calamity shall overtake us!' "[64] These are the false prophets "who cry peace when they have something to chew, but launch a war on him who fails to fill their mouths."[65] Jeremiah condemns the priests, the rulers, and the prophets for rebelling and ignoring God: "The prophets prophesied by Baal *and followed what can do no good*. The prophets prophesy falsely . . . but what I see in the prophets of Jerusalem is something horrifying; adultery and false dealing. They encourage evildoers, so that no one turns back from his wickedness.

To Me they are all like Sodom, and all its inhabitants like Gomor-
rah."[66] Jeremiah speaks directly to Hananiah: "Listen Hananiah! The
Lord did not send you, and you have given this people lying assur-
ances. Assuredly thus said the Lord: 'I am going to banish you from
the earth. You shall die this year, for you have urged disloyalty to the
Lord.' "[67]

Ezekiel declares that his denunciation of the false prophets came
to him directly from God. "The word of the Lord came to me: 'O
mortal, prophesy against the prophets of Israel who prophesy; say to
those who prophesy out of their own imagination. Hear the word of
the Lord! Thus said the Lord God: woe to the degenerate prophets,
who follow their own fancy, without having had a vision. . . . They
prophesied falsehood and lying divination; they said "Declares the
Lord," when the Lord did not send them, and then they waited for
their word to be fulfilled. It was false visions you prophesied and
lying divination you uttered, saying "Declares the Lord," when I
had not spoken.' "[68]

These and other references in the Bible to false prophets presented the laymen with the problem of distinguishing them from the
true prophets. Some tests are suggested. "And should you ask
yourself, 'How can we know that the oracle was not spoken by the
Lord?' If the prophet speaks in the name of the Lord and the word
does not come true, that word was not spoken by the Lord; the
prophet has uttered it presumptuously; do not stand in awe of
him."[69] This proposal that the answer to the question of divine
authority should be postponed until it had been demonstrated that
the prophetic message about a serious situation had come true
certainly does not help the man who is listening to decide whether
the speaker is a true or false prophet. It is asserting that the answer
to the question of true and false prophecy will be given in the
judgment of history.

There is another test which the Deuteronomist advances: "If
there appears among you a prophet or a dream-diviner and he gives
you a sign or portent, saying, 'Let us follow and worship another
God'—whom you have not experienced—and the sign or portent
that he named to you comes true; do not heed the words of that
prophet or that dream-diviner. For the Lord your God is testing you

to see whether you really love the Lord your God with all your heart and soul."[70] This warns against judging the authenticity of a prophetic message by some miraculous sign or wondrous performance. The real test is a matter of faith, of loyalty to Yahweh, and a devoted love for him. The answer lies in the message itself—does it confirm the faith of Israel's covenant with Yahweh? Is it in tune with what God had revealed at Sinai, to which their fathers pledged their allegiance?

Jeremiah recognized the false note in the prophecies delivered by the professional spokesmen for God—they failed to confront the nation with divine judgment upon the blatant disregard for justice, mercy, and humility. He suspected and denounced anyone who in the name of God assured the people that there would be peace and prosperity no matter how corrupt and debased were their lives. The authentic prophet confronts the people with God's judgment, he does not lull their spirits with rosy predictions of victory in battle and plentiful crops. The task of this prophet is not a pleasant one, and surely it was a very unpopular one. He was compelled to call upon his own people, whom he loved, to face up to their moral failures and their shameful disregard for the covenant with God which their fathers had made. Amos was applauded and cheered in Israel when he announced dire judgment upon Damascus, Gaza, Tyre, Edom, Ammon, and Moab for their brutal and brazen violation of all rules of human decency. This was Yahweh's true role—to punish Israel's enemies. But when the prophet turned to pronounce divine judgment upon Israel and Judah, they resented him and drove him out and told him to go back whence he came.[71]

The paid professional prophets conveniently brought a word from God which both king and people wanted to hear and approved enthusiastically. The genuine prophets, however, recognized them immediately and denounced them. A more difficult situation was presented by the earnest but deluded prophet who earnestly believed that God had spoken to him and given him a message for the nation. The integrity of these men was not at issue; their prophecies, however, were irrelevant and dangerous. Martin Buber suggested that the key to this ambiguous situation lies in recognizing the historical moment for the prophetic word. "It is not whether salvation or disaster is prophesied, but whether the prophecy, whatever it is, agrees with the divine demand meant by a certain historical situation, that is important. In days of false security a shaking and stirring word of disaster is befitting, the outstretched finger pointing to the historically approaching catastrophe, the hand beating upon hardened hearts; whereas in times of great adversity, out of which liberation is liable now and again to occur, in times of regret and repentance, a strengthening and unifying word of salvation is appropriate."[72] A sensitive interpretation of the historical situation determines the difference between true and false prophecy; the latter is recognized as a politician of illusion.

Hananiah was not an imposter, he sincerely believed in the divine origin of his message. His difference with Jeremiah was over the length of the Babylonian exile—he prophesied that it would end in two years, Jeremiah predicted a much longer period, seventy years. Hananiah based his prediction on the prophecy of an earlier prophet, Isaiah, who had declared that Jerusalem would never fall. [73] The sanctity and inviolability of the City of David was based on the fact that the Temple, looked upon as God's dwelling place, was there. Hananiah was only repeating what an earlier prophet had prophesied. His failure derived from his disregard of history, that times had changed. Buber credits Hananiah with a belief in a God of principles who would stand by earlier promises, and with a sincere patriotism which Jeremiah admired. The false note in his prophecy arose from his failure to be a realistic politician viewing the immediate historical situation before formulating God's message. He turned conditional promises into unconditional certainties. He was preaching his own desires, and projecting dreams as if they were reality.[74]

History is a distinguishing factor between true and false prophecy. It is in the historical event that God reveals his will to the prophet. Jeremiah said to Hananiah: "Yahweh did not send you, and you are causing the people to trust in a lie."[75] Overholt suggests that this may be paraphrased: "Yahweh did not send you in this particular situation, with this particular message."[76] The later prophet had to do battle against a misplaced security ascribed to God's Temple and holy city. This faith of an earlier prophet, even one as great as Isaiah, in God's unfailing protection of Jerusalem because it was the city of his holy house became irrelevant, and even dangerous, when it was invoked in a new and radically changed historical situation. It was unrealistic because it ignored the social and political condition of that moment. This nurtures a false hope which leads to disaster, as it did in the days when Hananiah and Jeremiah confronted the Babylonian threat to the nation. The false prophet in this case was not an imposter, although some of the professional prophets fitted that description. The false prophet may be a sincere man whose message is irrelevant to the historical situation of his time. He spoke the word of the Lord, but it was an old word which had been spoken in an earlier day, in a very different historical situation. Jeremiah was saying that in times that are rapidly changing, old prophecies, yes, even Isaiah's, were directed at the historical events of a past generation. They cannot be applied uncritically to a totally different situation. Hananiah was a false prophet because the message he brought was not from God speaking to the conditions of that moment in history.

Is the criterion of judgment between true and false prophets a relative one, dependent upon a concrete historical situation? Is the divine word different for different prophets at different times? Overholt suggests that Yahweh's dealings with his people were not exhausted in the positive action of the *Heilsgeschichte*, on the basis of which the people could rest assured and secure that God was on their side. Rather, Yahweh continued to confront them in their existence on the land, and to make demands upon them. How were these demands to be received if not through the instruction of the priests and the preaching of the prophets? And how were they to be evaluated if not through the decision of the people who weighed the content of each such interpretation in the dual light of an affirmation about their religious heritage and a knowledge of the historical situation in whch they lived? At its best a religious heritage cannot remain static, but must constantly be reinterpreted in the light of the people's changing situation in the world. [77]

Anton Boisen often said about hallucinatory voices assailing a hospital patient: "It is not that he hears voices, but what do the voices say? If they merely condemn everybody else, then he will get nowhere constructive. If the voices represent some criticism of himself, and suggest to what he should put his attention, then they may in a way be the voice of God."[78] In the case of the prophet, the validity of his claim that he heard God speak to him must be verified in the message he delivered. If it was in tune with the covenant God made with Israel, and if it was directed to the immediate historical situation, he is a true prophet. This gives him the authority to declare: "Thus said the Lord."

Chapter 3

Post-Biblical Views of Prophetic Authenticity

One of the puzzling phenomena of history is the abrupt end to which Hebrew prophecy came. It seems to have occurred after the Second Temple was rebuilt during the last decades of the sixth century B.C.E. The prophets who were active during these years, Haggai, Zechariah, and Malachi, were the last to be included in the canon. The Torah program which Ezra had introduced left no room for prophecy. God's will had been disclosed to Moses at Sinai for all future time. "This new community," writes Nahum Glatzer, "is built upon a spiritual order achieved by all: thus the interference of unpredictable enthusiasm granted a few is excluded."[1] Josephus and *Seder Olam Rabba* suggest that at the end of the Persian period the prophetic spirit departed from Israel, necessitating the final canonization of the sacred writings.[2] The Maccabeans, we are told, had no prophet at hand to tell them what to do with the stones of the polluted altar. They placed them in safekeeping until a prophet should appear.[3] Simon was made ruler and high priest "until a trustworthy prophet shall arise."[4] The same writer laments that it has been a long time since a prophet was seen.[5] George Foot Moore suggests that the author of that statement meant that no prophet had been seen since Haggai, Zechariah, and Malachi, with whom, according to Josephus and the rabbis, prophecy came to an end.[6] The psalmist sadly complains: "We see not our signs: There is no more any prophet; neither is there any among us that knoweth how long."[7]

A movement as old and dynamic as prophecy does not suddenly

disappear. Feeble remnants did linger for a while. Charlatans came upon the scene who so disgusted the people that all prophecy became disreputable. Zechariah describes the low estate it had reached. "If anyone 'prophesies' thereafter, his own father and mother, who brought him into the world, will say to him, 'You shall die, for you have lied in the name of the Lord'; and his own father and mother, who brought him into the world, will put him to death when he 'prophesies.' In that day, every 'prophet' will be ashamed of the 'visions' [he had] when he 'prophesied!' "[8] Men who claimed to speak out of ecstatic experience appeared in times of natural peril to deliver messages from God. Josephus wrote that during the time when Rome dominated Palestine, prophets and visionaries arose who predicted the fall of Jerusalem or promised its liberation.[9] "There are times," says Glatzer, "when Josephus himself assumes the role of prophet."[10] Prophetic thought manifested itself in some of the popular religious movements current at that time—gnosticism, mystic piety, and early Christianity. The position of authority which had been attained by scribes, scholars, and legalists was strong enough to phase out, and finally to bring an end to so historic and vital an institution as prophecy in Israel.

In a time of dark despair men tend to seek a supernatural intervention. The promise of the prophetic word that the suffering of the Babylonian exile would be followed by a bright future was not fulfilled. The study of Torah did not lead to a deliverance from the suffering brought upon all Israel by the oppression at the hands of the Greco-Syrian captors. A new phenomenon appeared for the first time in Israel which promised divine intervention directly after the period of suffering came to an end. A new form of revelation, Apocalypse, developed which was akin to the prophetic biblical writings, especially Daniel and Zechariah. Chapters 24–27 of Isaiah are probably the work of some later apocalyptic hand. The apocalypses which were collected are called pseudo-epigraphic, because the revelation was not made to the real author but to an assumed one, to one of the ancient saints or heroes of Israel. These share with the Biblical prophets a common concern for the future. The prophets saw the future arising out of the present, the apocalyptists saw the future breaking into the present. One projects history in evolutionary terms, the other expects a supernatural intervention. The prophets called upon the people to begin an inward moral transformation, bringing their lives into harmony with God. The apocalyptists inspired them with faith in an external power which would destroy the wicked nations and protect the righteous people. Both ascribed to God an active, participating role in history. The prophetic view discloses a divinely guided process of history leading gradually toward the messianic age. The apocalyptist, overwhelmed by the failure and defeat of human effort, embraces the sublime belief that Almighty God will directly and visibly intervene, and make immediately real the kingdom of God. The prophetic movement gave way to the apocalyptic as the disastrous conditions became more hopeless for the people.

In a foreword to the First Book of Maccabees A. A. Neuman writes that there is good reason to assume that the apocalyptic literature "strongly appealed to many sensitive, tortured souls, who could no longer find religious peace, or reconcile the prophetic promise with the stark realism of the wretched conditions under which the Jews lived in the Pre-Hasmonean period, either under the Ptolomies or Seleucids. It is out of the broodings of this deeply religious element that writings arose offering people a retreat to heaven, a flight to the mystic unknown. They stirred them with irrational faith in the immediacy of God's miraculous intervention in the fate of Israel."[11]

R. H. Charles attributes the origin of Christianity to this development. "It was from the Apocalyptic side of Judaism," he writes, "that Christianity was born—and in that region of Palestine where Apocalyptic and not legalism had its seat—even in Galilee."[12] The Rabbis during this period devoted themselves exclusively to the development of the oral law. The Pharisees were especially disturbed with the increasing popular interest in the Apocalyptic. They saw danger to the peace of Israel if Rome should recognize the hidden predictions for its destruction at the hands of the God of the Jews. Furthermore, the intense preoccupation with eschatalogical matters would divert the people from the present and the need to fulfill the divine commandments of the Torah. Scholars differ on the presence of apocalyptic thought in the Talmud and the Midrash. That there is some is evident in *Perek Helek*. In the main, however, there is more place for it in the mystic Jewish literature.[13] Primarily the Jewish tradition followed the Pharisaic judgment and rejected the apocalyptic view of prophecy.

The Rabbinic attitude toward the prophets was to accept them as disclosing that which had already been revealed at Sinai. They recognized only one revelation, *Torah M'Sinai*, that which God had spoken to Moses. The writings making up the prophetic literature, as well as the hagiographic, are not new revelations. They are, however, sacred writings, and at a late date were canonized into *Tanakh*, the Holy Bible. The Rabbis made extensive use of the prophetic writings. The list of quotations from Isaiah in the 250 pages of the *Mekilta* which Friedman edited fill three closely printed pages of the index. The Rabbis fully accept the prophetic writings into the canon as the word of God. They strongly rejected the suggestion that there could be another revelation from God following Sinai. The opening sentence of *Pirke Abot* makes it very clear: "Moses received the Torah at Sinai, and handed it down to Joshua; Joshua gave it to the elders; the elders to the prophets; and the prophets handed it down to the men of the great assembly."[14] There were some specific commandments which God had given to Adam, Noah, Abraham, and Jacob. However, to Moses alone did he give the complete revelation. All that followed, including the prophets, was intended only to explain and interpret the original. It could add nothing new; "nothing was kept back in heaven."

The rabbinic insistence upon one all-comprising revelation to Moses tended to lessen the authority of the prophets. The Talmud suggests that the prophets were not permitted to prophesy without the expressed permission of the Sanhedrin.[15] In the third century R. Johanan said that in the days of the Messiah, the books of the prophets and the Hagiographa were destined to be abrogated, but the five books of the Law would not be abrogated.[16] The Rabbis make it very clear that law is superior to prophecy, and that the sages take precedence over the prophets. Moses, as both prophet and lawgiver, was ranked superior to all other prophets. The position of sage is higher than that of king, a king above the priest, and a prophet must "bow hand and foot" to him. The five books of Moses possess greater authority than those of the prophets. The tradition accords Moses the highest rank. For the Rabbis, Judaism was Mosaism. He was for them the greatest prophet, lawgiver, and redeemer in the whole world. "The greatest redeemer, intermediary, intercessor, teacher, scholar, jurist, pious and righteous, 'the wisest of the wise, the greatest of the great, the father of the Prophets.' "[17]

In the talmudic literature the prophets are considered to be teachers rather than pneumatic personalities. Micah's call "to walk humbly with God" the Rabbis interpret as "to escort the dead to the grave, and the bride to the bridal chamber."[18] Deutero-Isaiah's plea to "Seek the Lord where he may be found," they say, means "in the houses of prayer and study."[19] The words which God put into the prophet's mouth they identify with the Torah.[20] The Rabbis believed that the prophets were engaged with them in a common task, the explanation of the revelation at Sinai and a call for its observance. Their approach to prophecy is to shear it of all uniqueness, to consider it as part of the universal revelation of God.

The Rabbis introduce terms which suggest that the divine revelation continues through a supernatural medium but does not supplant the authority of *Torah M'Sinai*. *Ruah-Ha-Kodesh*, "the Holy Spirit," is used to denote a universal indwelling of God in the world, his constant self-revelation to man. The *Shechinah* is the abiding presence of God by the side of man. Revelation in these instances is generalized and not limited to the prophets alone. In fact it is granted to a number of Biblical characters—patriarchs and matriarchs, Joshua, Rahab, Samson, Hannah, Samuel's son Joel, David, Solomon, and others. The *Ruah-Ha-Kodesh* is bestowed upon the entire people of Israel at the Red Sea, and at other times.[21] A fourth-century Rabbi said that when the people sinned with the Golden Calf, the *Ruah-Ha-Kodesh* departed from them and was replaced by a guiding angel.[22] The experience at the Red Sea elicited the comment: "The maid-servant at the Red Sea saw more than Ezekiel and all the other prophets. . . . that Ezekiel had only visions of God, but the Israelites at the Red Sea, as soon as they saw him, recognized him."[23] It appears that the Rabbis consciously strip the classical prophets of their unique position in revelation.

The Talmud records the case of the Rabbi who failed to convince his colleagues with his arguments and called for miracles from heaven to support his position. When heaven failed to respond, he appealed to the *Bat Kol*, the Heavenly Voice, and the miracles immediately appeared, allowing him to conclude that the *Bat Kol* confirmed his views. Rabbi Joshua, however, objected: "The Torah needs no heavenly voices. It was given at Sinai, and decisions are arrived at by following the vote of the majority."[24] In deciding the meaning of the revelation, supernatural forces should be ignored. If a sage predicted something, he did it not as a prophet but as one who learned it from his teacher. "I am neither a prophet nor a prophet's son, but I hold this tradition from my teacher."[25]

The disappearance of prophecy did not bring to an end the direct relationship between God and Israel. The divine will is made manifest through other means—the *Ruah-Ha-Kodesh*, the *Shechinah*, and the *Bat Kol*. All of these reveal to Israel what cannot be known through human knowledge. In the case of *Bat Kol*, the literal meaning is the resonance or echo of a human voice. "If a man calls to his fellow, his voice has a *Bat Kol*, echo, but the voice which came from the mouth of God [at Sinai] had no echo."[26] The Rabbis drew a clear distinction between the prophecies which were canonized in the *Tanakh*, the Holy Bible, and the communication which God has with Israel in their own time. "A voice came down from heaven, O Nebuchadnezzar, the kingdom is passed away from thee."[27] The king of Babylon cannot serve as a vessel for a divine message in the prophetic sense. The New Testament reflects this change: "And lo a voice from heaven, saying . . ."[28] A Rabbi of the third century compares Biblical prophecy to the presence of the king in the city and the message of God in a later period to a statue of the king. "The statue cannot do what the king himself can do."[29]

The Rabbis did not believe that God had ceased to speak to men in the post-Biblical period, but they understood it to be of a different order of communication. The prophet stood in the presence of Yahweh himself, who fashioned the message which the prophet delivered. He spoke only what God directed him to speak. The Rabbinic view of the qualifications a man must possess in order to receive a divine communication is significantly different from those which the Bible describes in the case of the classical prophets. The

Rabbis required that he study Torah and observe its commandments, that he perform good deeds and give charity. He must
prepare himself by study and good deeds. The Biblical prophets,
however, begin their careers in response to a divine call. "The
prophet," says Glatzer, "was moved by a divine pathos, he was
forced and controlled by a strong hand; his mission revolutionized
his life."[30] It is clear that for the Rabbis prophecy ended with the
biblical prophets.

There are several statements in talmudic literature which suggest
that the Rabbinic view of prophecy was influenced by the special
conditions in that period of Jewish history. When the sages were
gathered at Jericho, a mysterious voice said: "There is a man here
who is worthy that the Holy Spirit shall rest upon him, but his
generation is not worthy."[31] All eyes, we are told, turned to the elder
Hillel. A similar incident occurs at a gathering in Jamnia in which
the words of the mysterious voice are the same as in Jericho, save
that in this case they all turn to Samuel the Little.[32] These passages
are somewhat enigmatic, but they suggest that the Rabbinic leaders
refused to encourage the presence of anyone who could speak with
the authority of the Biblical prophets. In fact they had already
declared an end to the presence and work of the *Ruaḥ-Ha-Kodesh*:
"When the last prophets, Haggai, Zechariah, and Malachi, died, the
Holy Spirit closed out of Israel; but nevertheless it was granted to
them to hear the *Bat Kol*."[33] The Rabbis faced two dangerous threats
to their authority. The appearance of someone who arrives with a
special message from God can upset the orderly process of a society
based on revealed law as interpreted by qualified scholars. Biblical
prophecy is a threat to the tradition of Torah in a post-Biblical age.

A second and perhaps a more immediately visible threat was the
claim by the early church that prophecy had culminated in the Jesus
event.[34] The church understood the Hebrew prophets to be men
who foretold the future out of a unique and novel direct experience
with God. The Rabbis, on the other hand, understood those same
men to have been proclaiming what had already been revealed to
Moses at Sinai. In their view the prophets did no more than make
clear what Moses had spoken as both prophet and lawgiver.

The Rabbinic attitude toward prophecy was influenced, in part, by the polemic they were carrying on against the claims of the early church. The first Christians denigrated the Sinaitic revelation to Moses in favor of the writings of the Biblical prophets. It was in these writings that they read the prediction of the coming of Jesus as the Christ with a new proclamation of faith. They moved prophecy to the center of the religion of Israel and interpreted it to authenticate their claim that the church was the true Israel. [35] This arbitrary replacement of the Law of Moses by the prophetic writings aroused the Rabbis to great indignation and drove them to lose an objective position. They went so far as to question the effectiveness of the prophetic proclamations to change the nature or behavior of the people. They did not hesitate to remind the people that Moses prophesied for forty years yet failed to redeem Israel. Pharaoh "took the signet ring from his hand and put it on the finger of Joseph," who did redeem the people. [36] They pointed to the fact that Jeremiah's preachments were an abysmal failure in his effort to bring Israel to penitence. The Babylonian exile achieved that for the people. [37] "All the forty-eight prophets and the seven prophetesses were unable to lead them back to the right way, but the decree of Ahasuerus did." [38] This Rabbinic strategy of minimizing the role of the prophet in fashioning the character and destiny of Israel was, to a large measure, a response to the challenge which the early church presented. Commenting upon this Glatzer writes: "In these discussions the Talmudic teachers point to the primarily historic factors that accounted for the achievements denied the Prophets. It might be suggested that the Rabbis, particularly in the third century, emphasized the powers and authority of *historic reality* in an attempt to counteract the conceptions of the unconditional authority of the prophetic word." [39] Or as Dr. Bernard Bamberger in a personal comment wrote: "did they simply mean people can't take criticism; they learn only from adversity?"

A second element in the polemic which the Rabbis carried on against the early church centered around the prophetic announcement of God's judgment upon Israel because it had sinned against his Torah and covenant. Christian thought had placed the prophetic writings at the center of the Torah, and arrived at the unusual conclusion that Israel's sin was due to the failure of the Pentateuchal law. The Rabbis vigorously rejected the idea that the revelation came through the prophet. R. Huna suggested that the only reason there are more books than the five which Moses received at Sinai is that Israel's sin made it necessary. [40] The sages also took seriously the prophetic criticism of Israel for its sins against God and Torah. They differed, however, with the conclusions which the church drew from these same criticisms, as they differed from some which the prophets themselves had pronounced. The proposition that God will reject Israel and bring its history to an end offended the Rabbis very much. It is true that they had themselves spoken of the withdrawal of the divine presence in punishment for Israel's sins. But they never implied that this meant a final dissolution of the covenant which God had made with Israel. In this view, Israel is essential to the fulfillment of God's design for human history. To doubt that was, for the Rabbis, the supreme heresy. God does punish Israel when it violates the covenant, but it never occurs to them that Israel is not eternal, or that God can ever cease to love his chosen people. The claim of the church that God had forsaken Israel and had chosen a new Israel evoked from the Rabbis a vigorous reaffirmation of God's love for Israel and for its central role in the divine plan for history. God's love for Israel is unconditional, and their interpretation of the prophets makes that very clear. In the view of the Rabbis, God's destiny is inseparable from the fate of Israel. He suffers when they suffer, he goes with them into exile, he waits with them for the end of days, when "there shall be one Lord with one name." [41]

It is noteworthy that the Church created a dilemma for itself when it gave priority to the prophetic writings above the Sinaitic revelation. When it had established itself as an institution whose authority was vested in a head, or several heads, who ruled, the arrival of a prophet bearing a spontaneous divine message would be an embarrassment. Establishments have no room for a charismatic figure revealing a pneumatic experience outside the accepted order. The Church has continued to live with this dilemma, stressing on the one hand the centrality of biblical prophecy, and on the other hand rejecting the possibility of a new message from God through another prophet. Monotheism, which was essentially a prophetic movement, was condemned by the Church as a heresy. The Synagogue and the church have no room for a new genuine prophet. The moral of this may be that prophets cannot be at home in an institutionalized religion.

Philo Judaeus, an Alexandrian Jew of the first century, whose philosophic writings reflect Hellenic thought, described the Hebrew prophets as mantic in nature, supernaturally possessed diviners. Plato, in his *Phaedrus*, had suggested that for a man to receive a divine spirit, he must first be emptied of his human, or mortal, spirit. This prepares him to become a wholly passive instrument to be used by some greater power. His voluntary action performed by his normal faculties is suspended. This Platonic view of diviners or prophets is shared by most Greek philosophers. "No man achieves true and inspired divination when in his rational mind."[42] In his expository comment on the biblical statement: "And it came to pass that, when the sun was going down, a deep sleep [*tardaymah*] fell upon Abram,"[43] Philo, following the Septuagent, which reads "ecstasy" for "deep sleep," says that this suggests that Abram was divinely possessed, that he was in a state of frenzy (manic). He draws the conclusion that prophets as a class are all subject to the mantic experience. He goes on to say that "ecstasy is the experience of the God-inspired and the God-possessed" which proves him to be a prophet.[44] Wolfson writes: "To Plato, Scriptural prophecy is, in its essential nature, frenzy and ecstasy, a divine possession and an enthusiasm, and the Scriptural prophet with him one who is possessed by God."[45]

While he is in this mantic state the prophet receives a unique kind of knowledge, independent of sensation and the rational process. Philo wrote: "Some men are earth-born, some heaven-born, and some God-born. The earth-born are those who know only the pressures of the body, the heaven-born are men of science and art, and are devoted to learning, for the heavenly portion of us is in the mind. The God-born are those who have risen wholly above the sphere of sense perception, and have been translated into the world of the intelligible, and dwell there registered as free men of the commonwealth of ideas, and are imperishable and incorporeal."[46] Wolfson describes Philo's views this way: "The knowledge which the prophet receives and reports comes to him from another region, and is imparted to him by the divine spirit, and instilled into the rational soul of man, and therefore it takes the place of those rational concepts formed by the rational soul out of the data of sensation."[47] It seems clear that for Philo the prophet's words are never his own. He speaks only what God puts into his mind, which is wholly possessed by him during that time.

Philo's view of prophecy was strongly influenced by the Platonic-Stoic philosophies of Greece. The question which scholars have debated and continue to debate is the amount of Jewish-Hebrew sources he knew and read. He certainly knew the Bible in the Greek translation, the Septuagint. He was reared in a Jewish home where Hebrew prayers were recited, and the worship of the synagogue was in Hebrew. He refers a few times to rabbinic statements from Palestine. But there is no evidence that he was learned in the thinking of the Mishnah or Midrash. It would seem to be more of hearsay than actual knowledge.

What Philo understood when he spoke of the divine spirit which enters into the prophet is never answered by the philosopher. Wolfson draws upon references to it in connection with another discussion dealing with Philo's view of man, the incorporeal soul of man, and offers a theory. "It [divine spirit] is as a real being created by God after the order of angels, such as Philo's *divine spirit*, that the prophetic divine spirit is also conceived in native Jewish tradition where it is better known as *Holy Spirit*, or *Shechinah*, and it is also as such a being that the *Holy Spirit* started on his career in the history of Christian theology. The divine spirit is thus a sort of angel."[48] Wolfson also suggests that while Philo does not directly name this prophetic divine will *Logos*, there is ample evidence to warrant the possibility that the term does suit the idea.

In Judaism God can communicate his message through the *Ruah-Ha-Kodesh*, once he speaks, as in the case of Moses "face to face."[49] It has been noted above that God spoke directly to the biblical prophets, and the message they brought to the people was God's word fashioned in form and style by the personality of each prophet. Philo was aware of the scriptural prophetic experience. Commenting on the verse in Exodus (19:19), "As Moses spoke, God answered him in thunder," he raises the rhetorical question: "Did he do so by his own utterance in the form of a voice?"[50] The idea, of course, is absurd, since it suggests that God needs a mouth, and a tongue, and a windpipe. But the scriptural passage which tells of the revelation at Sinai clearly says that God spoke to the people, who heard a part of the Ten Commandments or all of them. This difficulty Philo resolved by calling upon a special miracle of a truly holy kind. God caused an invisible sound to be created, something incorporeal, living, and rational, in fact a rational soul full of clearness and distinctiveness. This invisible sound gave forth an articulate voice which was also incorporeal and yet is described as visible. This new miraculous voice was in action through the power of God which breathed upon it. The end result of all this was that it created in the souls of each of those present a miraculous sort of hearing which then went forth to meet the spoken word. This imaginative account of God's direct communication with a prophet was never intended to satisfy a twentieth-century mind. It is instructive here because it illustrates Philo's need to balance Greek philosophy with Hebrew prophecy. It was also called upon by a Jewish philosopher of the Middle Ages, as will be shown later.

The authenticity for divine revelation developed its own character as it moved through history. The Rabbis in the Talmud had brought classical prophecy to an abrupt end when they canonized the existing literature. They denied the classical prophets any claim to bringing a *new* message from God, confining them to what had already been revealed at Sinai. They did not reject the prophet's right to declare "Thus said the Lord" but insisted that what the Lord said had been spoken at Sinai. They introduced the *Ruaḥ-Ha-Kodesh,* the *Shechinah,* and the *Bat Kol* as intermediaries for divine communication. Philo took this development a step further and, under the influence of Hellenic thought, raised some questions about divine revelation which received serious examination by the Jewish philosophers of the Middle Ages. The influence of rationalism, as reflected in Scholastic philosophy, raised some of the earlier questions to a more critical point of inquiry. They began to ask whether it really made sense to believe that God actually communicated his will to a human being.

The Jewish philosophers carefully examined this question and arrived at the positive affirmation that God revealed his message to the prophet. Judah Halevi (1075–1141) and Moses Maimonides (1135–1204) shared a common ground of agreement on this matter, but they differed seriously about some aspects of it.[51] They agreed in their opposition to the Aristotelian view that God acts by the necessity of his nature. They understood him to act freely, in which there is an element of grace and election. They differed with each other on the method of divine communication; does it come directly from God to the prophet or through an intermediary? The Scholastic philosophers of that time conceived of prophecy as part of a natural process, arising naturally and inevitably out of certain conditions but not dependent upon divine grace.

Furthermore, the philosophers described divine communication in terms of indirect relationships, never direct. The intermediary was the Active Intellect, a real being, one of the incorporeal beings known as intelligences or angels. To qualify for the role of prophet, a candidate must be born with certain natural perfections. Through training he must also achieve perfection in moral and practical virtues; i.e., a perfect knowledge of arts and sciences. The man who passes these tests of mind and heart is qualified to prophesy without any regard for his allegiance to one or another religious practices. Any religion, any ethical system, or even a newly invented religion is acceptable. The philosophers were not parochial. Halevi and Maimonides responded differently to these definitions of prophecy which the philosophers advanced. Halevi, more poet perhaps than philosopher, rejected entirely the psychological foundations upon which the philosophers built their views of prophecy. He gave no credence to the existence of faculties in the soul which act as intermediaries. He accepted the religious aspect as primary, and prophecy as the direct creation of God's will. Maimonides, primarily a philosopher, accepted the thought that the divine message was mediated through the Active Intellect.

Modern man, reared in the cultural milieu of the sciences and philosophies currently in vogue, rejects the idea that intermediaries transmit a message from an incorporeal divinity to corporeal human beings. This kind of thinking belongs to an earlier age in man's

evolution, before he came of age. If, however, we are to take
seriously the prophet's declaration "Thus said the Lord," we are not
free intellectually to dismiss it cavalierly. Halevi, in his time, insisted that whatever it was that occurred when God spoke to the
prophet, it was a unique, distinctive, and unnatural event. Under
no circumstances could it be the end product of a natural process of
thought. He rejected outright the philosophers' proposition that a
prophet is a person who has achieved intellectual perfection. Mas-
tery in reason and logic, a knowledge of the arts and sciences, are
not prerequisites to the role of a prophet to receive a divine message. Halevi agreed that moral qualities are an essential requirement for a genuine prophet; he rejected, however, the vague description of them which the philosophers had prescribed. They had,
in a broad ecumenical sense, opened the gates of prophecy to men of
all religions, as well as to all ethical systems. Halevi was much more
particularistic. A prophet, in his view, is one who lives the life
prescribed in the revelation received by Moses at Sinai. Prophecy
for him was limited to the Jewish people, whom God had elected
because they had inherited from Adam a predisposition to prophecy. No other people is qualified for the office of prophet, not even a
gentile who converts to Judaism. Halevi pushes this particularism
even further, insisting that prophecy can take place only in Palestine. The prophets who spoke in lands outside the Holy Land
delivered a message which dealt primarily with Palestine.[32]

Halevi, like Philo, was profoundly impressed by the Biblical
account of the revelation at Sinai. In that event all the people of
Israel heard God speak even though they did not possess special
intellectual qualifications. It is true that they prepared themselves
in some moral and ritualistic practices. And yet, says Halevi, "The
people heard with distinctiveness the words of the Ten Commandments, which constitute the first principles of the roots of the Law,
. . . and these Ten Commandments were not received by the people
through the intermediary of single individuals or a prophet. They
heard it directly from God."[33] Philo had described the giving of the
Ten Commandments in somewhat similar terms: "These laws which
he gave in his own person, and by his own mouth alone . . . were

spoken by God with a clearness and distinctiveness, and reached the people in an articulate voice."[54] Halevi, like Philo, believed that what the people heard was not a voice produced by organs of speech. It was a miracle created by God for that special occasion. Unlike Philo, he does not go into the details of how the articulate voice came from the invisible being to the people who heard it. In the end, he writes: "We do not know how God's thought became corporealized, so that it was transformed into speech which struck our ear, nor what new thing God created out of that which had no existence, nor again what existing thing did he employ (in creating the new thing); for, all we know is that God does not lack power to do any of these things, just as he created the heavens and the stars by his will alone . . . and just as the water stood at his command, and shaped itself at his will, so the air which touched the prophet's ear was shaped into sounds of letters, which conveyed the thoughts to be communicated by God to the prophet and to the people."[55]

It has been noted previously that Scripture speaks of a *Ruaḥ-Ha-Kodesh*, a Holy Spirit, which comes upon the prophet at the time when he receives and then proclaims the word of the Lord. The Rabbis, in discussing this phenomenon, wrote that it implies a real being created by God. Halevi is aware of this tradition, but he interprets it to mean that God creates temporary, visible manifestations for the sole purpose of one particular act of communication with men. It is made especially for only one particular event, and should be distinguished from the Christian understanding of the Logos, or Holy Spirit, which is a permanent being. In the prophetic experience, as Halevi explains it, God shows the prophet certain spiritual forms which are made of that subtle spiritual substance known as the *Ruaḥ-Ha-Kodesh*.[56] Halevi decidedly parts company with the philosophers as well as with Christian thought, to take his place with those who understand prophecy to be a special gift of God free of all intermediary causes. If angels appear as bearers of the divine message, they are created specifically for this purpose and only for this one event. Indeed, whatever instrument God employs, be it angel, clouds, or spiritual forms, it is created to serve only one occasion, as God chooses. These do not possess an independent existence. In one place Halevi describes prophecy as a special stage of knowledge, the divine angelic stage, and the faculty by which that knowledge is attained he calls the divine faculty. [37]

Maimonides, whose views on prophecy reflect the influence of the philosophers, agreed with Halevi on one important belief— prophecy does not follow of necessity as a result of man's moral and intellectual perfection. "For we believe," he wrote, "that he who is naturally fit for prophecy, and has prepared himself for it, may yet not prophesy, for the art of prophecy depends upon the divine will, and according to my opinion, it is a miraculous act like all miracles, and it occurs in the same manner." [58] Prophecy, dependent upon the divine will, is not a direct act of God. He sends his *word* through the Active Intellect. "Prophecy, in its truth and essence, is a fire of grace flaming from God through the medium of the Active Intellect to man's rational faculty first, and then to his imaginative faculty." [59] The Active Intellect is the tenth of the incorporeal intelligences which guide the universe, and its assignment is the sublunar world.

To qualify for the role of prophet, Maimonides proposed that a candidate must possess two faculties—intelligence and imagination. Prophecy thus becomes a natural consequence which can be withheld from the prophet only by a miracle. God's role in this case is negative; he interrupts a natural process. A prophet in this case is a person qualified by intellect and imagination to receive a divine revelation which comes to him through the Active Intellect. Only God, by his own free act, can halt this natural process. Moses is the only exception, since he received the *word* directly from God, he heard *distinct words* at Sinai. [60] Maimonides rejected the views of Philo and Halevi, who believed that all the people had heard God directly when he spoke the Ten Commandments. What the people had heard, Maimonides wrote, was a *sound*, the meaning of which had to be explained by Moses. In fact, this indistinct sound the people heard only when the first two commandments were spoken; the other eight were inaudible to the people. Moses had to repeat them.

Like Philo and Halevi, Maimonides believed that the sound of the first two commandments was created by a miracle especially for that occasion, 'the created sound from which the intelligible word was

delivered."[61] Shlomo Pines wrote: "In other writings i.e. other than
the *Moreh Nebukim*, Maimonides describes Moses as having attained union with the Active Intellect; according to the conception
of certain Aristotelians, union with the Active Intellect represents
the highest goal, and is reached by the great philosophers."[62] The
ambivalence on this matter which Maimonides manifests is understandable. To exempt Moses from the natural process of revelation,
i.e., through the Active Intellect, would open the door to the
anti-rationalists. In his view the prophets were essentially philosophers, as was Moses. The difficulties which Maimonides experienced with the problem of revelation became intensified in the
modern world and brought forth the idea that the prophet was no
more than a very sensitive man who interpreted God's will as he
understood it. The *word*, it is said today, is of man and not of God.

Maimonides' disagreement with Halevi on the matter of the
non-Jewish prophet is inherent in his basic philosophy. The capacity
to achieve intellectual perfection and imagination is not limited to
Jews. "We believe a prophet or we reject him only on the ground of
the nature of his prophecy, and not on the ground of his descent."[63]
The Jews are not endowed with special qualities of prophecy that are
not shared by other people. The prophetic experience is universal
and is open to any person who achieves the perfection of mind and
imagination. When, however, Maimonides mentions the names of
non-Jewish prophets such as Job, Balaam, and others, he places
them in the second of the eleven categories or degrees of prophecy.
The first two degrees, he said, are not actually prophecy, they are
only "steps leading to prophecy." The scriptural non-Jewish
prophets, then, are not really prophets. If he happens to be called a
prophet, it is in the sense that "he is almost a prophet."[64]

Wolfson asks whether Maimonides believed that a non-Jew could
never rise above the second degree of prophecy. The fact that the
non-Jewish prophets he named are all assigned to the second degree
is no proof that they could not attain to a higher degree because of a
racial disqualification. There are *Jews* who do not get beyond the
second degree of prophecy, David, Solomon, Daniel, and others of
Jewish descent. The category they attain is not determined by their
being Jews or non-Jews, it is rather a matter of personal strength or

weakness. If there are no non-Jewish prophets in the highest category, it is because, like some Jews, they are not qualified by intellect and imagination. Maimonides remained true to his philosophic belief that prophecy is not limited to Jews, and if a non-Jew or a Jew is qualified to rise above the second degree of prophecy he does rise. The test is the same for both.

Although he had assigned priority to the perfection of the intellect over that of the imagination, Maimonides' commitment to the tradition compelled him to deal with scriptural and Rabbinic views of prophecy. "If there be a prophet among you, I, the Lord, do make myself known unto him in a vision, I do speak to him in a dream."[65] During the prophetic experience the limbs of the prophet tremble, physical strength fails him, his thought becomes confused. Scripture so describes what happened to Abraham, "and a deep dark dread descended upon him."[66] In that experience Abraham understands the message which God had given him. The prophets are described as full of fear and overcome by consternation, they become physically weak during the experience of prophecy. Moses is the only exception; God speaks to him as a man to his neighbor.[67] "Just as a man is not startled when he hears the words of his fellow-man, so the mind of Moses was vigorous enough to comprehend the words of prophecy while retaining his normal state."[68] This view of the ecstatic experience of the prophet reflects, in part, the teachings of Plato and Philo. Maimonides describes it as something terrible and fearful which the prophet feels while he is awake, in contradistinction to the dream experience. This is clearly described in the Book of Daniel: "So I was left alone, and saw this great vision, and there remained no strength in me; for my comeliness was turned in me into corruption, and I retained no strength."[69] Under such circumstances the senses cease to function and the Active Intellect influences the rational faculties, and through them the imaginative faculties, which then become perfect and active.[70] Maimonides differs from his predecessors on the subject of prophetic ecstasy in that for him the faculty of reason does not cease functioning during the time the prophet is experiencing it, and indeed, it is at that very time that the rational faculty is at its best.

The references in the tradition to the *Ruaḥ-Ha-Kodesh*, the Spirit

of Yahweh, or just the Spirit, which played an important role in
Christian writings and is present in both the Hebrew Scriptures and
the Talmud, find a very different interpretation in Maimonides from
what Halevi gave. Maimonides rejects altogether the notion of a
subtle spiritual substance, or the Neo-Platonic intelligible matter.
He understands these terms to be descriptions of the gift of prophecy, and more particularly denoting the first and second of the
eleven degrees of prophecy. Angels, in his view, are not formed of
matter and are permanent in their existence. He does take notice of
a reference to transient angels in rabbinic literature, but unlike
Halevi, he says that they are not real beings at all but refer only to
the physical and animal powers which guide and guard individuals
in the ordinary processes of life. [71]

The recollection here of the views of Halevi and Maimonides on
the nature and meaning of prophecy is important because it fore-
shadows the debate which the subject received in the modern
world. The philosophers of the Middle Ages, relying primarily on
Aristotle, conceived of prophecy as a natural process of the intellect,
and independent of God. This was a radically new confrontation for
the Jewish religious thinkers. A thousand years earlier, Philo followed the Platonic view, which conceived of the prophet as functioning while in a state of frenzy, during which time his mind was
emptied, and God filled it with his divine message. In that case God
used a passive instrument to deliver his will for men through the
prophet. In the Middle Ages, the Scholastic philosophers understood prophecy to be dependent upon a perfect intellect, which
really defines it as rational knowledge.

A twentieth-century mind recognizes in this view of prophecy of
the philosophers the beginnings of the school of thought which
defines prophecy as a natural phenomenon practiced by those
whose intellects are especially capable of comprehending the essential nature of the universe and of man. The Jewish philosophers
outrightly rejected the natural-process theory of prophecy, in which
God acts by the necessity of his nature. In that view God always acts
in freedom, and if there is a process it is dependent upon the will of
God. They differ with each other on the question of how God
functions in prophecy. Halevi believed that divine revelation comes

as a direct communication from God to the prophet. Maimonides conceived of it as passing through an intermediary, the Active Intellect. This debate between the Scholastic philosophers and the Jewish religious thinkers is a prefigurement of a later religious controversy over whether the prophetic message is of God or of man, whether it comes directly or through an intermediary.

Every generation lives in modern times, but is not much impressed with the fact. The Elizabethans considered themselves very modern in contrast to the ancients. "This awareness of a shared newness," wrote Crane Brinton, "of a way of life different from that of one's forebearers, and by 1700 of a way of life felt by many to be better than their forebearers—this is itself one of the choicest marks of our modern culture."[72] The chief characteristics of our modernism derive from the Enlightenment, which began with the end of the Thirty Years War in 1648 and culminated in the French Revolution at the end of the eighteenth century. In cultural terms it was initiated when Francis Bacon published his *Novum Organum* in 1620, and attained its high point with the issuance of Kant's *Critique of Pure Reason* in 1781. The Enlightenment brought together the humanistic spirit of the Renaissance and the scientific revolution of the seventeenth century.

One of the important characteristics of the new era was the emancipation of man's mind from domination by theology. Human intelligence began to supplant divine revelation. In the seventeenth century the philosopher Descartes laid the foundation for this radical change with the declaration that reason is a basic principle of knowledge. Furthermore, he proposed the thesis that the application of analytical geometry can resolve all problems. Truth, he argued, is achieved through the method of rational deductions derived from *clear ideas*. All notions are subject to critical rational examination. The authority by which men had been guided in the past was now threatened, and the traditions in which they had lived securely came under suspicion. A line had been drawn marking off the medieval from the modern. The mind of the individual was accorded the responsibility to determine certitude, and to function as if religion did not exist. Descartes had arrived at his view of the world by a process of deduction on purely rational grounds. This

world, it turned out, is a machine created by God, operating autono-
mously on mechanical principles. Animals in this view are machines, or automata; men in their bodies are also machines. There is
one exception—men have souls.

The primary question in religious thought is epistemological; i.e.,
how does man know God? Historically two answers had been given
to the question. Man knows God through revelation, or he knows
God through reason. The philosophers of the Middle Ages resolved
the issue by harmonizing faith and reason. They defined revelation
as a body of knowledge communicated by God to man, some part of
which can be obtained independently, or at least verified. In the
thirteenth century St. Thomas Aquinas described it as "an ascent of
the natural light of reason through created things to the knowledge
of God . . . and a descent of the miracle of revelation, of divine truth
which exceeds the human intellect, yet not as demonstrated to our
sight, but as a communication delivered for our belief."[73]

Maimonides, a century before Aquinas, had prepared the philosophic foundation for the harmonization of faith and reason. In his
view, revelation required of man that he use his intellect not only to
understand what had been revealed, but to attest to the certainty of
revelation itself. Strauss puts it succinctly:

> Revelation itself summons those men, suitable for the task to philoso-
> phize. The divine law itself commands philosophizing based on this
> authorization, takes all that is as its object. Revelation as the Law
> given by God through a prophet becomes the object of philosophy in
> prophetology. Were revelation *merely* a miraculous act of God it
> would be entirely beyond man's comprehension. Revelation is then
> understandable only insofar as God's act occurs by means of interme-
> diaries, taking place in creation, in created *nature*. In order fully to be
> understandable it must be plainly a natural fact. The means used by
> God in the act of revelation is the prophet, i.e. an unusual and
> superior human being, but nonetheless a *human being*. Philosophical
> understanding of revelation, philosophical confirmation of revelation
> is thus the elucidation of prophecy from the *nature of man*.[74]

The peaceful coexistence of faith and reason endured so long as
the philosopher was free or perhaps even required to philosophize.

In an age of belief, says Strauss, the philosophers "justified their philosophy before the forum of the Law; they derived from the Law's authorization to philosophize the duty to do so."[75] Spinoza, Descartes, and those who followed upset this peaceful arrangement. In the three succeeding centuries they reduced faith to the position of a subservient handmaid to reason and experience. The paradox of this situation is demonstrated by the strange views of Descartes himself. As a rationalist he proceeded as if religion did not exist. But, as a man of faith, he wrote a letter to Mersenne in 1630 saying, "God, as creator, created all eternal truths. He is creator of the essence of things, as he is the creator of the reality of things. He created as Monarch (absolute), even the law of contradiction. God can make two plus one not equal three, and he can make a mountain to exist without a valley."[76] The claim of reason in this monarchial absolute power of God is a paradox indeed. Tacitly Descartes decided in favor of reason. Pascal saw through all of this: "I cannot forgive Descartes; he would have been very pleased had he been able in all his philosophy to avoid giving the Creator a part here in the world; but he could not help allowing God a tap on the world with a finger in order to set it in motion, and having done so, he had no more need for the Creator."[77]

Spinoza avoided such paradoxes. Reason in his view had undisputed authority in man's search for truth. Revelation he assigned to the domain of obedience or piety. "The power of reason does not extend so far as to determine for us that men may be blessed through simple obedience without understanding. This is what revelation tells, and indeed tells us nothing else . . . defining the dogmas of faith only in so far as they may be necessary for obedience and leaving reason to determine their precise truth."[78] The sharp distinction which Spinoza drew between faith and reason, faith dealing solely with will and observance, while reason bears total responsibility for determining truth, plays a major role in the development of religious truth in the modern world. In the eighteenth century, for example, Moses Mendelssohn advanced this as the basis for the religion of the Jew. Dogmas, he wrote, are arrived at through reason, which is universal. Practices are revealed in legislation and are accepted by faith. Revelation and prophecy in the Biblical sense are excluded by this system of thought.

Spinoza did not explicitly discard the traditional view of the divine origin of Scripture, but, as Guttmann suggests, it "is so formulated that the philosophic impossibility of the concept of revelation is apparent."[79] The supernatural is contrasted with man's natural illumination. The possibility of prophecy is placed beyond human reason. To understand the prophet we must rely on the words of Scripture themselves. Prophecy, belonging to the realm of the supernatural, is of necessity an impossibility. A miracle is impossible because the order of nature comes with absolute necessity from the divine essence. Anything which happens contrary to this order conflicts with our certain knowledge of God. The idea of revelation or prophecy defies this natural divine order. Spinoza reserved revelation for the realm of eternal truth, never for legislation. The ignorance of the recipients converts this truth into commandments of specific laws and deeds. Israel, including the prophets and Moses, confused the revealed truths when they turned them into statutes and laws. He denies the possibility of divine legislation. To speak of revealed religion is to deal with fantasy. Unlike Maimonides, who understood prophetic inspiration to depend upon the prophet's faculties of reason and imagination, Spinoza confines prophecy to the imagination. He assigns to the prophet the role which Maimonides had assigned to the soothsayer. In his view religion is to philosophy what imagination is to knowledge.[80]

The publication in 1690 of John Locke's *Essay Concerning Human Understanding* rounded out the basic structure of Enlightenment thought, which dominated philosophy until the anti-intellectual reaction in the post–World War I era. Its two distinguishing characteristics were a rebellion against all authoritarianism, and the emergence of individual conscience and reason as the primary arbiter of truth and action. Describing the nature of a lover of truth, Locke wrote: "One unerring mark, viz. the not entertaining of any proposition with greater assurance than the proofs it is built upon will warrant. Whoever goes free beyond this merit of assent, it is

plain . . . loves not truth for truth's sake, but for some other end."[81]
The attribution of autonomy to man is complemented by an en-
larged view of reason which extends beyond Descartes' speculative
and abstract definition. Following upon Bacon's *Novum Organum*,
Locke added the experimental method to the basic rational instrument in the search for truth. Empiricism became the intellectual
handmaiden of rationalism. The inductive and the deductive
processes of thought were made available to future philosophers.
Kant and Hume, among others, called upon both of them in building their philosophic systems.

Locke described three categories of truth, one of which is contrary to reason. First, there is the truth which accords with reason
and is discovered by tracing ideas from sensation and reflection, and
by natural deduction is found to be true or probable. Then, there is a
truth which is above reason—a proposition whose truth or probability cannot be derived from reason or experiment. And then, there is
that which is contrary to reason—such propositions which are inconsistent with, or irreconcilable to, our clear and distinct ideas. The
existence of God, for instance, is according to reason; the resurrec-
tion of the dead is above reason; the existence of more than one God
is contrary to reason. "I say that the same truths may be discovered
and conveyed down from revelation which are discovered by reason. . . . So God might by revelation discover the truth of a proposition of Euclid. In all things of this kind there is very little need or use
for revelation, God having furnished us with natural and surer
means to arrive at the knowledge of them. For the knowledge we
have that this comes from God, can never be so sure as the knowledge we have from clear and distinct perception of the agreement or
disagreement of our own ideas."[82]

Faith, then, is ascribed to those truths which cannot be attained
by reason. The statement that part of the angels rebelled against
God and thus lost their first happy state, or that the dead shall rise
again, "these and the after-life being beyond the discovery of reason
are purely matters of faith, with which reason has directly nothing to
do."[83] The uneasy tension in which Locke maintained reason and
faith is evident in his writing that "Whatever God hath revealed is
certainly true, no doubt can be made of it. This is the proper object

of faith; but whether it be a divine revelation or no, reason must judge; which can never permit the mind to reject a great evidence to embrace what is less evident, nor allow it to entertain probability in opposition to knowledge and certainty. There can be no evidence that any traditional revelation is of divine origin, in the words we received it, so clear and so certain of the principles of reason. And therefore, nothing that is contrary to, or inconsistent with, the self evident dictate of reason, has a right to be urged or asserted to, as a matter of faith wherein reason has nothing to do."[84] He advanced the proposition that faith is dependent upon the "credit of the proposer" as coming from God in so "extraordinary a way of communication. . . . This way of discovering truth to men we call revelation."[85]

Locke asked the critical question in the matter of prophecy—how reliable is the prophetic claim to declare "Thus said the Lord"? How shall we judge the "credit of the proposer" who asserted that the message he is about to deliver came to him from God? The one piece of testimony which is wholly unacceptable is the enthusiasm of the spokesman as a substitute for reason. His description of the enthusiast is perceptive and, to a degree, touched by mockery. "The enthusiasts are those who cannot be mistaken in what they feel . . . they are sure because they are sure, and their persuasions are right only because they are strong in them. But, to examine a little soberly this external light, and this feeling on which they build so much, the question here is—how do I know that God is the revealer of this to me, that this impression is made upon my mind by His Holy Spirit, and that therefore I ought to obey it?"[86] In Locke's view the enthusiast is caught in an insoluble dilemma—he claims the veracity of revelation because he firmly believes it, and he firmly believes it because it is a revelation!

The seventeenth-century philosopher's criticism of the enthusiasts merits a full quotation.

> Light, true light, in the mind is, can be, nothing else but the evidence of the truth of any proposition; and if it is not a self-evident proposition, all the light it has or can have is from the clearness and validity of those proofs upon which it is received. . . . God, when he makes the prophet, does not unmake man. He leaves all his faculties in their

natural state, to enable him to judge of his inspirations, whether they
be divine or original or no. . . . if he [God] would have us assent to the
truth of any proposition he either evidences that truth by the usual
methods of natural reason, or makes it known to be a truth which he
would have us assent to by his authority, and convinces us that it is
from him by some mark which reason cannot be mistaken in. . . .
Every conceit that thoroughly warms our fancies must pass for an
inspiration, if these be nothing but the strength of our persuasions
whereby to judge of our persuasions. If reason must not examine their
truth by something extrinsical to the persuasions themselves, inspirations and delusions, truths and falsehoods will have the same measure, and will not be possible to be distinguished. Thus we see the
Holy Men of Old, who had revelations from God, had something else
beside that eternal light of assurance in their own minds to testify to
them that it was God. They were not left to their own persuasions
alone, that those persuasions were from God, but had outward signs
to convince them of the Author of those revelations.[87]

Devastating as this passage is to the enthusiasts who believe
because they believe, it is somewhat unclear about the "outward
signs" which proved to the prophet that the message was truly a
revelation from God. It is evident that Locke does make room for
miracles, limited to be sure, in his view of the relationship of God
and man. "It is to be considered that the divine revelation receives
testimony from no other miracles but such as are wrought to witness
his mission from God who delivers the revelation. All other miracles
that are done in the world, how many or great whatsoever, revelation is not concerned in."[88] Neither Descartes nor Locke resolved
the inconsistency of their rational commitments and their religious
faith. They were much more persuasive in their philosophy than in
their theology.

In addition to the autonomy of the individual in reason and
conscience, and the empirical method as an instrument in the
search for truth, the Enlightenment introduced a new attitude
toward nature. Isaac Newton, mathematician and physicist, and a
contemporary of Descartes and Locke, advanced the proposition
that what is natural is reasonable. The laws of nature, he found, were
orderly and uniform, always and everywhere the same. Following

upon this, it was asserted that the same laws which applied to nature were operative in human affairs. Beneath the divergencies of outward appearances there lies a universal principle. Institutions such as monarchy, the church, and society were described as *unnatural* because they had destroyed man's freedom and corrupted his natural integrity. The social and political movement which began to examine the credentials of the existent social structure had its roots in the Enlightenment philosophy. It became known as liberalism, and played a major role in the disappearance of feudalism, autocracy, and supernaturalism. Kant defined, in what for him is colorful language, the meaning of the Enlightenment: "[It] is man's release from self-incurred tutelage. Tutelage is man's inability to make use of his understanding without direction from another. *Sapere aude!* [Dare to know.] Have courage to use your own reason! That is the motto of the Enlightenment."[89]

The philosophy of Immanuel Kant dominated the intellectual and moral thought of the eighteenth and nineteenth centuries. He had proposed separating pure reason from practical reason. The exercise of theoretical reason cannot lead to any such knowledge of supersensible reality as religion requires. "I must therefore abolish knowledge to make room for faith."[90] The absorbing human enterprise during this period of history was the conquest of the globe upon which man dwelt. The rationalism of Descartes laid the intellectual foundation for this exciting activity. His success with it encouraged man to rely upon himself and his reasoning faculties. Kant's philosophic system gave expression to man's growing confidence in himself as a rational being. It is described as a Copernican Revolution, implying that it helped to move the center of gravity from the world to man. In Kant's view, God becomes a postulate of moral reason, since we cannot possibly know him through pure reason. God is "a regulating principle of reason, directing it to see all the relations in the world *as though* they are derived from a necessary cause. . . . Furthermore, we think, as if the world, its existence and internal determination, flowed from divine intelligence . . . and when I say that one has to see the world as though it were the work of divine intelligence and will, I am merely stating that as the clock, the boat, are related to the watchmaker, the ship builder, and the commander, so is the world of our senses related to the unknown."[91] Kant's writings disclose that in his view God occupies a secondary place. Commenting on Kant's moral deism, Hans Ehrenberg wrote: "The cosmological deism of Newton ejected God from the visible world, and provided him with a refuge in creation as a prime mover or legislator of the laws of nature. God was made *Honorary Chairman of Nature*. Similarly, moral deism does the same thing, it appoints God *Honorary Chairman of Morality*."[92]

The Enlightenment thinking on the subject of God and his relationship to man culminated in the philosophy of Kant, who opened new vistas of understanding. It projected God as a useful hypothesis, a necessary one, *eine notwendige und dienlich Annahme*. A postulate nevertheless. Kant's major concern was man and humanity. The practice of praying to God he characterized as nothing but "madness arising from superstition" or "the making of fetishes." Humanity, however, is significant, yes even sacred.[93] The post-Kantians transformed the general mood of their master into a doctrine. Fichte and Schelling withdrew from God the denomination of absolute, the *aesitas*, that which is underived being. That title they bestowed upon man, whom they described as absolute Ego. The Ego exists, therefore, only by virtue of itself, and it is given as that which is unconditioned. So the Ego becomes the creator of the world, and the entire world is immersed within the Ego. In the face of such thinking, it could no longer be affirmed that God really exists. It was suggested, instead, that he comes into being in an ongoing process. Indeed, mankind is God on the way toward his final coming into being. The proposal that God does not exist as reality, but that he is dependent upon man, who allows him, in a gradual process, to come into being, gives strength to the individual Ego to continue to exist. "This view of man as God coming into being, and God as the god of man's destiny gives Fichte's philosophy its great pathos."[94]

In *The Instruction for a Life of Happiness*, Fichte argues that we cannot answer the question, What is God?, so long as we cleave to a shadowy view of God. "If we could know God as He is in Himself, face to face, do not seek Him beyond the clouds. He can be found in every place where you are. Look upon the life of his devotees and you will see Him; devote yourself to God and you will find Him in your heart. . . . The awareness of the absolute unity between human existence and the existence of the divine is the deepest awareness that is given to man to attain."[95] Bergmann's comment on this passage is: "Clearly in this system there is no place for God in the traditional sense of the word. . . . The philosopher has no God, and it is inconceivable that he should have one. God cannot be an object, for then He would be conditioned by the Ego, like all objects."[96]

At the close of the eighteenth century, the Enlightenment philosophy had been completed. It seriously challenged the dogmas of the established religions. It demoted theology from the high office of Queen of the Sciences, assigning her an honorary but unimportant place in the intellectual hierarchy. The throne was now occupied by reason, science, and nature. These now decided what truth is, and what faith is. Many philosophers had played a role in this intellectual process. David Hume, who usually prefaced a statement with "Unless I am mistaken," contributed substantially to it. He recognized the difficulty one faces in the attempt to distinguish between true religion and superstition. He made a polite concession to the philosophic mood of the time by proposing that the universe was a creation by something analogous to the designing mind.[97] However, such attributes of God as providence, immortality, and the biblical story of the Fall on the Day of Judgment he described as superstition. The proposition that a prophet spoke words which God had revealed to him was he argued, the work of the prophet's imagination, or his capacity to deal with fantasy. The intellectual climate as the nineteenth century dawned found orthodox believers adhering to the traditional dogma of divine revelation as recorded in Scripture. The cultural movement which Descartes had set in motion robbed the biblical view of prophecy of a respectable hearing by those who were now convinced that truth, including religious truth, must pass the test of reason and science.

The experience of the Jew during the period of the Enlightenment differed significantly from that of the Christian. The ghetto had isolated him, and sheltered him from the rational-empirical philosophy which characterized the intellectual climate of the seventeenth and eighteenth centuries. The Jew lived secure in the Maimonidean assurance that his faith in the revelation at Sinai was valid and reasonable. The new ideas of Descartes, Spinoza, and Locke did not pierce the ghetto walls. It was not until Moses Mendelssohn (1729–1786) came from Eastern Europe to Berlin that the first confrontation took place between the Enlightenment and the Jewish tradition. He became aware of the growing conflict between *Torah M'Sinai* and the rational-empirical philosophy currently popular. Spinoza had resolved this conflict by confining religious truth to the test of universal reason while assigning Torah to the realm of political guidelines for Israel. Since Israel was no longer a political entity, there was no need for either Israel or Torah. Few Jews, if any, were aware of Spinoza's solution to the Jewish dilemma. His excommunication by the synagogue had deeper roots than those popularly charged against him. In Spinoza's view, Jews had no reason for further existence.

Mendelssohn accepted half of Spinoza's resolution of the conflict between revelation and reason. He agreed that the truths of religion are arrived at through reason, which is common to all men, and are, therefore, universal. Metaphysical matters—God, freedom, and immortality—may be known only as we reason our way to them. Torah (revelation) is wholly outside the rational process. Judaism, as Mendelssohn viewed it, is not a revealed religion, it is a revealed Torah, which is legislation. The sole function of Torah is to guide people toward eternal truths. The laws, at best, "allude to or are undergirded by the eternal truths, or they recall and stimulate thought about such."[98]

Mendelssohn managed to live religiously comfortable in both worlds—the universal religion of man arrived at by reason, and the special community of Torah revealed to Israel. He preserved human reason and divine revelation by divorcing them. This tender balance did not, as it could not, long endure. The orthodox segment of the Jewish community was not especially disturbed by the separation of religion from legislation. They preferred the view of Maimonides, which taught that the Torah was both revealed and rational, the religious principles and dogmas along with the observances and practices. However, they could live, without serious protest, with Mendelssohn's program of separation so long as the laws, the *mitzvoth* which they were required to obey, were divinely commanded.

Jews who were persuaded by the liberalism of the Enlightenment were not hospitable to Mendelssohn's dichotomy between religion and legislation. If reason is the only method of discovering religious truth, why should it be discarded in the case of law and observance? Many liberals began to doubt revelation altogether. Two cultural developments shook the traditional view that the Bible was divinely revealed, a new critical reading of Scripture, and the publication of Darwin's *Origin of Species*. A critical reading of the Bible disclosed that it was written by different groups of Jews at different times, and that it contained errors, contradictions, and irrelevancies. This had been hinted at by ibn Ezra in the Middle Ages and was more elaborately discussed by Spinoza, the first modern. In the nineteenth century, however, the evidence from philological and historical studies was demonstrating that the biblical text ascribed to revelation could never have been given by God to Moses at Sinai. Furthermore, Darwin's description of the evolution of man was in direct conflict with the account given in Genesis, which was, in the new day, declared to be a myth. At the end of the nineteenth century, divine revelation and prophecy were being seriously questioned. Those who refused to apply the rational-empirical method to the study of religion retained, and still retain, the view of a supernatural origin for the Bible and religion.

The last chapter of Enlightenment thought was written by a group of philosophers at the University of Marburg described generally as Neo-Kantians. One of the leading spirits among them was Hermann Cohen (1842–1918). He was the son of a cantor, and a Hebrew teacher. He studied at the Breslau Seminary for the training of rabbis. He left these Jewish studies and began a serious study of philosophy, and finally received his doctoral degree from the University of Halle. Early in his philosophic work he recognized the inadequacy of the Hegelian doctrine of absolute idealism. It seemed to him that it disregarded the growth of science and the reality of practical life. Cohen was no less in protest against the philosophy of materialism, which stressed the primacy of the physical sciences but

neglected the subject of the nature and destiny of man. He proposed, instead, the thesis that pure thought is ultimate reality.

Kant had taught that the materials of which the world is formed
are sense impressions. Thought, in his view, is a synthesis, a creation of the connection between sense impressions which are given.
Cohen rejected this Kantian thesis and argued that thought itself
produces everything out of itself. Sensation merely describes the
problem posed by thought. Color and sound, for example, are
beyond man's senses. Physical theories are not confined to sensation. "Sensation stammers," he wrote, "thought must first supply
the word; sensation denotes the dark impulse, but only thought can
illuminate its direction."[99] Thought, in this case, produces its object,
and logic becomes the primary science because it leads to pure
thought, which is *being*. Thought and being are one, that which is
not *being* is *becoming*. Thus, in Cohen's view reality is not something given (datum), it is present as a task. Ideas, in the Platonic
sense, are creators of the foundations of being. An idea has its origin
in itself, and the only demand made upon it is consistency, which
calls for logic, the primary science. "Reality is never reached," he
wrote, "it is an infinite task that is never attained, the final goal of a
journey that is never completed."[100]

In a similar vein, Cohen discusses the nature of man and the
ethical reality which should govern his life. Man, he contends, is not
a zoological specimen, a *homo sapiens*, which are categories that
treat with the individual. Man cannot be understood in these terms
because the individual is an integral element in the totality of men,
which is indivisible. In himself, an individual human being has no
existence; only the community is a reality. History validates this
proposition, Cohen argues, if we examine the development of human society from the clan to the tribe to the nation, progressing
until it ends in humanity as a whole. In this case, then, ethics is the
product of reason, not of experience. It begins with *ought*, which is
the *idea* of being. The important point in this thesis is that we must
deal with the idea of man, not with his psychology. As the process
moves toward the realization of the pure idea, the ultimate ought, it
approaches closer to the goal—mankind.

The Neo-Kantian view of reality complicated the problem of

prophecy for the twentieth-century religious thinker. Cohen introduced God as the idea that makes possible the relationship between
being, which is pure thought, and will, which is the ought of ethics.
God is the bridge between nature and man, he is the source, the
origin of both the world of nature and the world of values. He is the
unifying force. "Every endeavor of ethics which is made without
God, is bereft of thought and principle."[101] God, then, is the guaran-
tor of morality by maintaining nature for its fulfillment. He is an
idea, a necessary idea, but not a reality. God is not *being,* he does
not exist, he cannot be described, and he need not be believed in. To
know God one must reason his way to him. This view of God
presents problems which are not relevant to our discussion of
prophecy. However, God as the idea which guarantees man's moral
efforts does present difficulties to anyone trying to understand
revelation or prophecy in terms of modern culture. Later in his life
Cohen found his own view inadequate and advanced the thought
that God is the being to which all else is becoming. Interesting as
this is, it does not lessen the challenge to prophecy which the
Neo-Kantians presented. Theologians and philosophers had to take
a more critical look at the biblical claim of God's revelation to Moses
and at the meaning of biblical prophecy.

In the middle of the nineteenth century, Benjamin Jowett coun-
seled students of religion: "Interpret the Scriptures like any other
book. There are many respects in which Scripture is unlike any
other book. . . . The first step is to know the meaning, and this can
only be done in the same carefree and impartial way that we ascer-
tain the meaning of Sophocles or of Plato."[102] This advice was more
radical when it was given than it is today. If the book containing the
revealed word of God is to be subjected to a critical examination by
the newly acquired disciplines of historiography and linguistics, it
may turn out that the Holy Book is factually inaccurate, that it
contains contradictory statements, and that the discoveries of science categorically deny the account of creation as written in the
Book of Genesis, and thus the belief in divine scriptural revelation
may be put in jeopardy. Furthermore, if God is an *idea* instead of
reality, as the rationalists were teaching, then the assertion by a
prophet that he speaks the word of God is open to very serious

doubt. Theologians were challenged to interpret the prophetic "Thus said the Lord" to a generation conditioned culturally to read the Bible like any other book.

The first response by some liberal interpreters of the Bible was to describe the prophet as a man who was inspired in much the same sense that an artist is and had a special genius for an experience with God. The first chapter of this book has already discussed the creative artist and the prophet of God. A second response was directed at a change in the very nature of the divine message itself. The traditional view had described it as a special communication from God to the prophet spelled out in human language. Some modern religious interpreters discarded this and advanced the proposition that the prophet understood the will of God in the historic events of his time. The experience of the exodus, the victories of Assyria and Babylon over Israel, and other historical events commonly known were, for the prophets, acts of God in which his nature and, more important, his will are revealed. The setting for the prophet's encounter with God was a historical event. He does not speak of God in metaphysical terms, although, at times, he describes God's moral nature. He is never the philosopher offering a series of propositions which lead to faith. Instead, he points to a historical event of common knowledge which he interprets with a special insight granted him as a prophet.

The modern biblical interpreter began to define prophecy as a natural phenomenon. The supernatural mystery which enveloped it, and which lay beyond human comprehension, was relegated, along with other myths, to the days before man came of age. The proposition that there is a divine message in the events of history can be examined by the canons of reason. The presence of men especially gifted to experience God's role in history does not offend against the rational mind. It is probably universal for most men to have ears that hear not, and eyes that see not. The creative poet and artist prove that to us every day. A prophet uniquely sensitized by faith to hear God, and to interpret the meaning of life and history out of that experience, presents no problem to the modern mind.

The classical prophet is never described as a passive vessel into whose mind flowed the word of God. Jeremiah was keenly aware of his role: "Assuredly, thus said the Lord: . . . if you produce what is noble out of the worthless, you shall be my spokesman."[103] The prophet is saying that the authenticity of his message depends upon his subjective decision, and the loyalty to it that he demonstrates. It is the prophet who chooses the word of God and commits himself to it. The biblical prophets had no Scriptures to guide them; all they had was a nomadic tradition orally preserved. Coleridge said: "Whatever finds me, bears witness for itself that it has proceeded from a Holy Spirit."[104] The prophet, like the poet, is certain that whatever ultimately *finds* him is the authentic voice, whether of God or the muse. Origen, in the third century, understood it. "He who with diligent attention reads words of the prophets will from his very reading experience a trace and a vestige of inspiration himself, and this personal experience will convince him that these are no compilations of men, which we are firmly persuaded are the words of God."[105] The subjective, intuitive ingredient is essential to prophecy, and for those who read it. This, as has been said before, is also characteristic of art and those who view it.

The intelligent modern believer learned to live comfortably with the new view of prophecy. Revelation through history, nature, and man can pass the test of reason, a primary requirement for the enlightened mind. The seemingly inexplicable mystery of God speaking in human language was resolved when the emphasis was shifted from the speaker (God), to the hearer (man, prophet). The archbishop of York, William Temple, described the new understanding of prophecy in these words: "For them [Luther and other great reformers] the word of God was a living, present utterance of the living God to the souls of men, spoken through, rather than contained in, the printed Bible, and its divine quality was vindicated by the *testimony of the Holy Spirit* in the heart and conscience of the reader."[106] This twentieth-century churchman has taken us a considerable distance from the traditional view of prophecy, which held that God had spoken every word precisely as recorded in the Bible. The prophet, in the new view, is described as one who reads God's message in the events of history. The printed word is not literally the word of God.

"In the light of modern thought," wrote Samuel S. Cohon, "the traditional conception of revelation must be modified by stressing the human element in the receptivity of the divine message, and the consequent fallibility which that inescapable factor engenders. However, the belief in revelation as a progressive process whereby the Creator's activity, thought, and purpose are disclosed to spiritually gifted souls, remains pivotal to Judaism."[107] The prophet, then, does not receive a message of divine words ordered for his delivery to the people. Rather, he is aroused by the presence and will of God in a particular situation. The language he uses to phrase the divine command is in the particular idiom of his people, and in the literary forms native to it. The profound experience with God in these events gave rise to predictions which the prophet made concerning the future of Israel. Because of the strong human element in his prophecy, it was not free of error.

Modern religious thought humanizes prophecy when it shifts the emphasis from God to man. The prophet is described as one especially prepared to recognize the divine in the secular. The message he delivers did not come full-blown from without into his empty mind, any more than scientific truth comes to the scientist wholly from the outside. In both cases there is preparation which enables them to comprehend a new truth. Jeremiah was a profound student of human affairs to the same degree that Einstein was a keen student of the laws of nature. Both were also gifted with the quality of genius which enabled them to see more than the average student. The prophet, prepared and spiritually gifted, disclosed to the people the meaning of a historical event and predicted its consequences in the future. Amos understood his role when he said: "Indeed, my Lord God does nothing without having revealed his purpose to His servants the prophets."[108]

The creative scientist reveals a new understanding of nature in a somewhat similar process. Sir W. R. Hamilton, the discoverer of quaternions, was walking and talking with his wife when "an electric circuit seemed to close, and a spark splashed forth, the herald (as I saw immediately) of many long years to come of definitely directed thought and work, by myself if spared, and at all events, on the part of others, if I should ever be allowed to live long enough distinctly to communicate the discovery."[109] Sir William, the scientist, was well prepared for that moment when "a spark flashed." Years of training and research had preceded it. He relates that he could not resist the temptation to carve his famous formula into a stone of the bridge on which he was crossing; "Just as a prophet was often moved to the symbolic act which expressed and also initiated the larger activity to come. This instinct to make visible the invisible, probably belongs to all creative work, and goes deep down to the very object of divine creation to bring forth in a new realm and category something that already exists, but is not yet revealed to man."[110] The similarity between the prophetic experience and those of creative artists and scientists helps the rational religious believer to come to terms with biblical prophecy. There is, however, a very critical difference which has been alluded to earlier in this book. The prophets were certain that the source of their message was God. The word they spoke, while fashioned by them in rhythmic form, and rooted in their intellectual activity, was the authentic word of God. The artist and the scientist is unaware of the source of his inspiration. A secularly oriented mind finds the claim of divine origin for prophecy a stumbling-block. This will be faced in a later portion of this work.

It is noteworthy that science itself acts upon presuppositions in its work. That there is a world exterior to our minds, which can be known to our minds, cannot be proved, it may only be acted upon as a hypothesis. The uniformity of nature which the scientist finds in his work is possible only if he presupposes that the uniformities are a reliable sample of nature as a whole. He proves the uniformity of nature by assuming that it is uniform. When the church fathers say, "I believe in order that I may know," they are not indulging in obscurantism. They are, in fact, describing the nature of all knowledge. We must have faith in the possibility and value of truth before we can set out to find it. There is a *faith principle* which must precede thinking. Whitehead formulates this view succinctly: "The dogmas of religion are attempts to formulate in precise terms the truths disclosed in the religious experience of mankind. In exactly the same way, the dogmas of physical science are the attempts to formulate in precise terms the truths disclosed in the sense perceptions of mankind."[111]

The twentieth century has witnessed a vigorous rebellion against modernism and liberalism in religious thought. Once again, prophecy underwent a radical reformulation and interpretation. Karl Barth, a pioneer in this revolt, began by drawing a sharp distinction between the words of the Bible and the word of God. The Bible, he believed, contains only the words of man, suffering the weaknesses and limitations of any human activity. However, these words in the Bible have the potential of *becoming* the words of God, but only by the grace of God, and in the power of the Holy Spirit. They become the word of God whenever God speaks his word through them. "The Bible is to its being in this becoming what the tiny word *is* relates in the statement that the Bible is God's word."[112] The word of God is never something which can be analyzed, catalogued, or defined; it is not something to be understood through research or reason. The word of God is a concrete act of God, a miracle, an event which depends entirely upon the grace of God. The Bible is the record of God's word spoken to different men on various occasions. These words speak to us only when God freely chooses to give us his word. The text is not God's word; it becomes God's word only when a man takes it seriously, waiting until he hears the voice of the prophet. In Barth's view, then, God reveals his word at the time and place he chooses, man can only read the text and wait in faith until God speaks to him through it.

The complaint the neo-orthodox theologians leveled against the humanization of prophecy which the liberals had introduced was that it "threw away the pearls because they are covered with sand. This is what the rationalist does; . . . in freeing himself from the blind authority of Scripture."[113] To find God's word in the Bible one does not go poking around in it with critical reason. What man knows rationally is not the word of God but the general timeless truth. The liberals looked upon the Bible as a document of religion which in itself has no meaning for faith. "It is," says Brunner, "an historic or aesthetic object, an object of my admiration, like the Egyptian pyramids, but it has nothing final to tell me. Nobody has anything final to tell me save God Himself in His word."[114]

Those who in this neo-orthodox spirit *listened* to the word of God in the text of the Bible did not discard the critical-historical method of interrogating it. Bultmann maintained that the Bible is a historical document, and as such it is subject to examination by the science of history. To those who protest this view and contend that the biblical writings are affirmations of faith and proclamation, Bultmann answers that if they are to be understood as such, they must be interpreted historically, "in as much as they speak to us in a strange language, in concepts of a far away time, of a world picture that is alien to us. Put quite simply, they must be translated, and translation is the task of historical science."[115] The historical method is necessary if we are to understand the text in its historical setting. It, however, does not lead us to the word of God, which appears only if we are prepared always to hear it anew, and to ask for it in every decision of life. "The Bible does not approach us like all other books; it claims at the outset to be God's word. We did not come across the Bible in our cultural studies, as we came across, for example, Plato or the Bhagavad Gita. We came to know it through the Christian Church, which put it before us with authoritative claim. . . . It says, 'God speaks to you here! In His majesty He has chosen this place! We cannot question whether this place is the right one; we must listen to the call that summons us.' "[116]

Contemporary man is not attuned to hear the word of God when he reads the Bible. For many it is a book of religious writings which they read either mechanically or solemnly as an act of piety. Students examine it with a critical-historical analysis as a source for the history of religion or civilization. It is currently fashionable to study the Bible as literature, searching it for aesthetic views. Martin Buber describes modern man's interest in the Bible as a "subdivision of a detached spirit, which will fail us as one must fail it. If we seize upon it as the expression of a reality that comprises all of life, we really grasp it, it grasps hold of us. But contemporary man is scarcely capable of this grasp any longer."[117] To hear God speak through the Bible, a man must know it as a *thou*, as a sign of the inner essence of God. Only those who know God can hear him. The central point of post-liberal religious thought is the conviction that God's word can be heard only by faith. The *thou* of faith cannot be proved in another person, nor in God. "Reason of itself, " wrote

Reinhold Niebuhr, "cannot prove the truth of revelation, but given the revelation reason can show that it gives a more adequate picture of reality than any alternative."[118]

This brief survey of more than two thousand years of searching for an answer to the mystery of the prophets' proclamation "Thus said the Lord" has disclosed a variety of responses. The Rabbis denied the prophet any claim to having received a unique and special message from God. What the prophet speaks, they maintained, had already been revealed to Moses at Sinai. The medieval philosophers introduced the Active Intellect as an intermediary between God and the prophet. The modern liberal humanized the prophetic experience to the point that it is more the word of man than of God. And the theologians in the postliberal period reversed the trend; they returned the word to God, who could grant it at his will. We appear today to be no nearer a resolution to this very old mystery. If it was beyond the comprehension of men who were more or less of religious faith, how shall a generation steeped in secularism—i.e., living as if there is no God—understand the divine word as a credible reality? To describe the prophetic message as a noble social vision or as great moral poetry is to rob it of its fundamental character, for as has been emphasized in an earlier chapter of this book, the prophet's major claim is that he spoke the word of God. It is interesting, and perhaps revealing, to learn that the biblical prophet himself was aware of the dilemma which men who listened to him had with his claim to announce "Thus said the Lord." Isaiah complained: "So that all prophecy has been to you like the words of a sealed document. If it is handed to one who can read, and he is asked to read it, he will say, 'I can't, because it is sealed,' and if the document is handed to one who cannot read, and he is asked to read it, he will say, 'I can't read.' "[119]

Chapter 4

Theism: Classic and Neoclassic

The prophetic faith culminated in the prophecies of Deutero-Isaiah, the last of the giants of classical prophecy. He spoke to the Babylonian exiles when homesickness was followed by their awe and wonder at the achievements of Babylonian civilization as compared to the rustic culture of their own small land. It was at this time that the Babylonian study of the heavens was attaining the status of a real science. "Before the astonished Jews," wrote Professor Irwin, "there was unfolded a world of immensity, of wonder, and of regularity such as to render ludicrous the traditional claim that Yahwe, god of the tiny land of Palestine, had made not alone the sun and moon, but the host of the stars also."[1] The prophet realized that this was the moment to make clear the meaning of the claim that Israel's God is God.

> Who measured the waters with the hollow of his hand,
> And gauged the skies with a span,
> And meted the earth's dust with a measure,
> And weighed the mountains with a scale
> And the hills with a balance?
> Who has plumbed the mind of the Lord,
> What man could tell him His plan?
> Whom did He consult, and who taught Him,
> Guided Him in the way of right?
> Who guided Him in knowledge

And showed Him the path of wisdom? . . .
Lift high your eyes and see:
Who created these?
He who sends out their host by count,
Who calls them each by name;
Because of His great might and vast power,
Not one fails to appear.[2]

Ethical monotheism best describes the prophetic faith, and was most fully recorded by the poetic prophet of the exile. It presented the belief in the one God of the universe who is the creator and sustainer of all that exists. He directs the course of human events in accordance with moral laws which he had made part of creation. He chose Israel to be his witness to all the people of the earth. "I the Lord, in My grace, have summoned you: I created you, and appointed you a covenant-people, a light of nations, opening eyes deprived of light, rescuing prisoners from confinement, from the dungeon those who sit in darkness."[3] This faith was fashioned in the cultural climate of nearly three thousand years ago. It was radical for its time, and for some even heretical.

Questioning the validity of classical theism upon which the prophetic faith was founded did not come full-blown into the modern world. The previous chapter briefly discussed the postbiblical critical examination of its authenticity from the period of the rabbis to the medieval philosophers and into the Enlightenment and the final effort of the neo-orthodox and existential thinkers of the modern world. It appears that every age asks the religious question in terms of its own culture, and must seek for an answer within those terms. There is, of course, a logical continuity with the understanding of previous ages. The Hebrew prophets lived in an era which Karl Jaspers calls the "axial period of history," a time when radical questions were being asked, and nontraditional answers were proposed. Confucius, Buddha, Zoroaster, and the Greek philosophers were engaged in a similar enterprise which set human history upon a new cultural road.

The religious question is the same for all ages; i.e., what is the meaning of human existence? Primitive man answered it in terms of the culture of his time—animism, totemism, fetishism, and taboo.

The Pantheon of the ancients mirrored the lifestyle of the Greeks. Classical theism, which began with the Hebrew Bible and was acceptable until the twentieth century, presented a view of God who is supernatural, omnipotent, and omniscient. "Culture," says Malinowski, "is the artificial secondary environment which man superimposes on the natural. It comprises language, habits, ideas, beliefs, customs, social organization, inherited artifacts, technical processes, values."[4] As these vary and change, man's response takes on innovative and different expressions. Man cannot be said to lose faith when the current formula no longer informs his life. The religious response to the meaning of human existence must be intelligible within the culture to which it addresses itself. Religion disappears as an active phenomenon when it fails to heed the demands of cultural development.

The present cultural climate is, largely, not receptive to the classical view of the universe. Van Harvey defines this view as referring "to a system of thought in which is postulated EXISTENCE of one unified, perfect being that, although distinguished from the cosmos, is the source of it, and continues to sustain it, in its form and powers, and, in some sense, providentially, guides it."[5] The idea that there really exists an ultimate, perfect, unchanging, supernatural being who is self-sufficient, adequate to himself without need of all else, an uncompromising absolute, is rejected by the secular, scientific view of the universe which dominates the culture of modern man. There is also an inner inconsistency in the idea of a supernatural God who is perfect and independent of his creation while at the same time requires of men that they freely obey him; he in no sense needs them, and is himself unaffected by whether they do good or evil. The atheist pays his respects to this classical view of God by asserting that his denial of its truth is the rejection of all theism. "Whenever it abandons a system of thought," says Lubac, "humanity imagines it has lost God. The God of *classical ontology* is dead you say? It may be so; but it does not worry over much . . . and if classical ontology disappeared, it was surely because it did not correspond adequately with being. Nor was its idea of God adequate for God. The mind is alive, and so is the God who makes himself known to it."[6]

It became clear at the beginning of the twentieth century that the liberalism which characterized the culture of the modern world is naive in its view of human nature, and innocent about the dynamics of human history. It committed a very critical error when it applied the rational-empirical epistomology to the entire cognitive sphere, which the logical positivists enshrined into dogma. It neglected dimensions of human experience which the scientific-rational method can neither investigate nor explain. Aesthetic reality, for instance, is for physicists *mere appearance*, which consigns an important segment of human experience to unreality. Religion suffered a similar fate when its claim to truth was subjected to a test alien to its nature. The question of the meaning of human existence is not the subject matter of either science or ethics. Stephen Toulmin suggests that there are limiting questions which arise at the limits of our moral and scientific inquiry. After all the conventional answers have been given to our moral questions we are still confronted with the limiting question—why should I be moral at all? Questions of the same type arise at the boundaries of scientific explanation. It is to answer these limiting questions that Toulmin assigns religion. "Ethics provides reasons for choosing the right course, religion helps us to put our hearts into it."[7] Erich Fromm supports this view in psychological terms: "All men need a frame of orientation which is a more fundamental need than sexuality, social power, and possessions. Man has a craving for knowledge of the right direction."[8] Religion's primary function is to satisfy that craving.

In protest against this embarrassing failure of the rational-empirical epistomology, neo-orthodoxy and existentialism arose as the road toward the answer of the limiting questions. These were still within the liberal tradition in their rejection of the claims of orthodoxy. One substituted an authentic sense of scriptural witness, the other the legitimacy of the experiential in place of logic and science as a response to man's quest for the meaning of human existence. The variations on these new themes are many and illustrate the validity of William James's *Varieties of Religious Experience*. Kierkegaard pointed to radical paradoxes, Schleiermacher spoke of the feeling of absolute dependence, Barth stressed the experience of revelation in the word, Tillich emphasized ultimate concern, and Buber found reality in the I-Thou. Each of these, and there are others, is unique, but for our purposes here they may be catalogued under the general rubric of philosophy of life, usually associated with Dilthey, Bergson, and especially with James's radical empiricism. Heidegger summed up the existential view: "The foundation of all man's experience is his awareness not only of the being of others as essentially related to his own being, influencing and being influenced by it, but also of his own unique existence as radically free and responsible."[9]

This philosophy-of-life program served as a strong protest against the monopolist claims of the rational-empirical epistemology of yesterday's liberalism. However, it too proved itself inadequate to lead men toward an answer to the religious question as modern secular man asks it. It speaks of God in terms of ordinary existence whose reality is ultimately a personal experience. Liberalism, in neither of its dimensions—empirical-rational and neo-orthodox–existential—satisfies modern secular man's search for the meaning of his existence. A tragically staggering price has been paid for this failure. As the modern age passes into the postmodern, the remarkable success of the rational-empirical epistemology in the physical and social sciences left unexplained important areas of human experience, and religion is one of them. In his secular pursuits man has shaped his view of the world in scientific terms; he found the secular a success. Unfortunately, and unexpectedly this led to secularism, which eradicated anything beyond the secular, beyond what science and mathematical logic can validate. Thus man finds himself today living in a crisis which in Whitehead's words is a "foreground with no background."

The event which more than any other separates the modern world from the postmodern and which compels us to reevaluate our basic understanding of man's place in the universe is the fission of the atom. This ushered in an axial point in human history; matter is no longer material, since the atom is formed of protons, neutrons, electrons, and twenty or more other particles. We cannot ask what these particles are *made of*, since they are not *substance*. We speak of energy, waves, particles, but what we are actually dealing with are fleeting episodes in the microcosm which are not permanent. Our picture of reality, then, is not yesterday's matter, but today's relationships, processes, and events rather than bits of substances. Instead of an edifice of hard building blocks, ultimate reality is relational. The primary entities are gregarious and integrative, uniting into more complex structures. Protons and neutrons form atomic nuclei, which unite with electrons to form atoms, which then attach themselves to other atoms to form molecules. These in turn conjugate, becoming matter in bulk, moving then into crystal, rocks, mountains, planets, galaxies, and the universe or universes. The universe, then, as we know it today is made up of gregarious elements which stick together. Harry Schilling writes: " . . .the dynamism of this relationality displays remarkable developmental drives—so that matter itself may be said to be constructive and developmental—it builds."[10] Reality, then, begins with relation.

Along with relationality, indeterminacy is an integral character of matter. Alternatives and chance are inherently part of reality. Quantum physics demonstrates that there are several possible states a system may occupy. Only in large numbers of identical systems does predictable behavior arrive, and it becomes more determinate in a statistically significant sense as the number and frequencies of occurrence increase. The universe could have had many histories other than the one it has had. Something else could have been and was not. For five or ten billion years each stage of history has been a springboard for the next, with many possible directions in which the jump could be made. These basic characteristics of reality—relationality and indeterminacy—comprise a unitary, integrated whole of systemic interdependence, solidarity, and common destiny for all of its inhabitants and components.

The metaphysics which most satisfactorily accounts for the nature of the universe as disclosed by the New Scientific Revolution was formulated by Whitehead. It basically rejects the sensationalist doctrine of Descartes and the Enlightenment with its presentational immediacy or world sense. Instead, Whitehead begins with the experience of the self, which is aware of past bodily and mental states, as well as of the world beyond itself. On the surface this shares something of existential epistemology but is unique because it also asks a critically new question—what is the dominating insight whereby we suppose ourselves as actualities within a world of actualities? Whitehead's answer begins with a nonsensuous perception, a mode of awareness more basic than sensation, so that we know ourselves as creatures in a world of creatures. The metaphysics which supports this advances the proposition that "at the base of our existence is the sense of worth. It is the sense of existence for its own sake, of existence which is its own justification, of existence with its own character."[11] Here, then, there is something that matters, which is to say that reality is something that matters.

Cognition in this case begins not with substance, but with self-enfolding fellow-creatures as well as the infinite whole in which we are somehow included as one. The ONE is compelled in experience which is relational and monistic at the same time. Infinitude is an inseparable part of the finite. The value of human existence, then, lies beyond ourselves. In this view reality, comprising ourselves, others, and the whole, is the *sense of deity*, or as he describes it, the *intuition of holiness* which is the foundation of religion. The reality of God is inescapable as long as we experience that whole of which we are a part, and which we trust. Schubert Ogden defines it concisely: "*God* is the very meaning of *reality* when this word is defined in terms of our basic confidence in the significance of life, and the kind of questions and answers such confidence make possible."[12]

Creativity and infinite freedom are integral to the universe, in which there is also a realm of forms with infinite possibilities. "These forms and this creativity," writes Whitehead, "are together impatient to achieve actuality apart from the completed ideal harmony, which is God, who is the final mode of unity, in virtue of which there exists stability of aim amid the multiple forms of potentiality, and in virtue of which there exists importance beyond the finite importance for the finite actuality."[13] It is suggestive, perhaps even significant, that John Dewey, writing from the perspective of comprehensive empiricism, expressed a metaphysical view somewhat similar to that of Whitehead. "Every act," he writes, "may carry within itself a consoling and supporting *consciousness of the whole* to which it belongs, and which in some sense belongs to it. Within the flickering, inconsequential acts of separate selves dwells a sense of the whole which claims and dignifies them. In its presence we put off mortality and live in the universal."[14] Unlike Whitehead, Dewey did not pursue the consciousness of the whole to the ONE. His use of the word "God" refers, as with James and other pragmatists, to an idea which is affective and effective. Commenting on the use of the word "God," Bertrand Russell said: "I can respect the man who says that religion is true, and therefore ought to be believed, but I can feel only reprobation for those who say that religion ought to be believed because it is useful, and to ask whether it is true is a waste of time."[15]

The truth claim for the existence of God as a reality cannot be validated for secular man by any mode of classical theology. The religious question—i.e., the meaning of human existence—remains unanswered in the postmodern age either by orthodoxy or liberalism. The more the scientist discovers about the world of nature, the more, it appears, remains to be examined and explained. He does all of this without any recourse to God, substituting science for mythology. Empowered with sophisticated technology, he possesses increasing ability to understand as well as to control the world, and increasingly the universe, he inhabits. The God hypothesis of classical theology, which purported to fill the gaps in nature that man could not explain, has become invalid for secular man today.

Julian Huxley, one of the few scientists with a literary flair, wrote: "God is beginning to resemble not a ruler, but the last fading smile of a Cheshire cat. . . . It will soon be impossible for an intelligent, educated man or woman to believe in a God as it is to believe that the world is flat."[16] The claim that God acts in history as classical theology describes it does not make sense to the historian or the scientist today. The waters do not part when God blows upon them, and the Assyrians do not attack Israel at God's command. Camus in *The Plague* has the priest call upon the people to repent and to resign themselves to God's will. The doctor, however, rejects the idea that God had anything to do with the coming of the plague or that God can bring relief from it. As a doctor his job is to use his medical knowledge to relieve human suffering.

These and similar protestations against the role of God in nature

and history do not, in themselves, constitute a denial of his existence. They represent, in most instances, a rejection of a particular
theistic scheme common to a different cultural era. What is dead
today, in this age dominated by science, is the classical view of God
who is "up there" or "out there" managing the world as he wills.
History records many reformulations of man's view of God. The
Biblical prophets did not reject God when they radically altered the
priestly view of him. But their own theism was rooted in a theology
which described God as supernatural, omnipotent, and a being who
acts directly to move the course of history. The mood of our postmodern culture is inhospitable to this classical theism in which God
can either cause a holocaust or prevent it from happening. It is well
to keep in mind the probability that the neo-classical theism which
expresses the metaphysics of the New Scientific Revolution appears
adequate for the present. It is, however, not the final, unchanging
view of God. The future will probably look back upon it as a step
forward in the ongoing process of history.

Avowed atheists sometimes give unacknowledged testimony to
the existence of God. Sartre insisted upon responsible humanism in
a world in which "It is absurd that we are born, it is absurd that we
die."[17] Julian Huxley, who had preached the funeral sermon over
faith in God, confessed his inability to explain away experiences like
those of "an awareness of transcendental power, communion with a
higher reality, a sense of sacredness."[18]

The most formidable attack upon theism in the modern world has
come from the Stalinist-Maoist Marxists. Their plans to build a
utopian future call for the elimination of capitalism, imperialism,
and religion. They are dedicated to the achievement of a humanitar-
ian society for all men everywhere in which cooperation and
sacrifice are integral factors. Their case has merit so long as religion
is defined in classical theological terms. But if God refers to the
objective ground of reality, as neo-classical theism maintains, then
the goal, hope, and commitment of Marxism is another unacknowledged testimony to the existence of God. Modern secular man
reveals not a distrust in God but a rejection of the classical formulation in which God is presented—Karl Barth's assertion that "if we
ask why creation, or each of us, or everything has to be as it is, the

answer is that it must be by God's free will."[19] This is unacceptable to a man whose view of the universe is fashioned by science, which has no room for an omnipotent deity who acts in history without the participation of either nature or man. It is not God who is unacceptable, but Barth's neo-orthodox theology.

The Midrash relates that Moses went down to earth to visit a class in which Rabbi Akiba was explaining the Torah to his students. He was unable to follow the complicated hermeneutics and felt himself a stranger to this world of Torah which God had revealed to him at Sinai. He was about to leave the class when he heard Rabbi Akiba say: "This is the Law given to Moses at Sinai." He realized that Rabbi Akiba's world, however strange it might seem, was the proper offshoot and descendant of what he, Moses, had wrought at Sinai.

This rabbinic story recognizes the fact that the Torah tradition would undoubtedly have disappeared if it had not been critically appropriated by each new generation in terms of its own historical situation. There never has been, nor can there ever be, a traditional theism, because the change in metaphysical schemes causes the form of the theistic image to change. "The Scriptural tradition is the only constant in the situation. But the matter of Scripture becomes a living word only when interpreted by people in their own situation. There is no revealed metaphysics. There is no single metaphysics of theism."[20] There is one caveat which must be observed in this continuous process of interpretation—the essential core of meaning must remain unchanged. The form can be altered if it is to be alive in history, the responsibility which falls upon each generation is to distinguish wisely and faithfully between the essential meaning and the inessential form.

Ethical monotheism is the heart of the prophetic faith and is based upon the covenant which God made with Israel at Sinai. The prophets did not invent it. They interpreted it, and reinterpreted it, to make it relevant to new historical situations. They never discarded the spirit of the original covenant in which the fundamental principles were spelled out. They couched it in the language and form of the biblical age, portraying God, among other characteristics, as one who acts with a stern moral will and who is the Lord of history. "When the ram's horn is sounded in a town, do the people not take alarm? Can misfortune come to a town if the Lord has not caused it?"[21] "I form the light and create the darkness, I make weal and create woe, I the Lord do all these things."[22] No matter how appealing to modern secular man is the ethical message, the theological frame in which it is framed is unacceptable.

A principle of openness characterizes the prophets' approach to the covenant. They felt free to criticize the popular view of God which tradition had preserved and protected. This freedom introduces the possibility that their own theological formulation, as well as any other, may be critically examined and, if found wanting, may be altered or even discarded. This openness allows men to question and reformulate the existent theism only if the spirit of the original covenant is preserved. This rules out atheism, or what is popular today—secular humanism. Ethics without God violates the essence of the covenant to which God and man are partners. The neo-classical theism which was presented earlier in this chapter is readily appropriated by the prophetic faith, since the essence of the covenant is retained. Postmodern culture comfortably accepts it; in fact it strongly supports it. Relationality is at the very heart of the prophetic faith. "The prophetic idea of God," wrote Martin Buber, ". . . is an expression of man's longing for rescue from his own inner duality."[23] The Biblical command that "Thou shalt love the Lord thy God" is meaningless unless there is in man a desire to be reunited with his origins. Love can never be demanded, even the love of God, unless it is directed toward finding oneself in unity with the ONE who is the unity of all that exists.

The reality of God is unavoidable once we begin our thinking with the self as part of the organic nature of the universe which is visible to everyone. What is not immediately self-evident is the nature of God and how he functions. Four propositions which are integral to the postmodern view of the universe may guide us in our search for possible answers. The first, which has been discussed above, describes reality as a unified whole, or *one*. This supports the prophetic claim for the truth of monotheism. Within this one reality, it is clear today, there exist elements of change, mind, creative freedom, and cosmic purpose. The classical clear-cut distinction between transcendence and immanence has been made irrelevant by the new scientific picture of the relativity of time and space as well as of external and internal. The reality of the ONE, God, is supreme and ultimate, but never beyond; infinitely more than anything observable in us, and in the cosmos. At the same time God is part of reality, not apart from it. In neo-classical theism God is best understood by the term "transcendent-immanent." The unity of the ONE is emphasized by the simultaneity of human experience.

A second proposition which is inherent in the new view of the universe which science has revealed is the fact that all known reality, including God, is relational, not absolute. The universe seems to be an ecosystem in which all parts are interrelated, interdependent, and interpenetrating. No one part exists in isolation; it is affected by, and itself affects, all others, and the system as a whole. God is part of this relationality, and his being depends upon what happens in the uncertainty of time. What God will be is *contingent*, in large measure, upon what man does. God is the eminently relative ONE, and being relative to all others is himself relative to nothing. God is the absolute ground of any and all relationships, his own and all others. God, being the most relative, is therefore the most absolute.

A third proposition declares that God is personal, not abstract. A human person is a knowing, willing, caring unity in continuity. A self-identical unity endures as the person changes. God is also self-identical even though he changes. He is not a unity of other beings, however related to them he may be. Like man, God changes, but the unity in continuity persists. He prehends all; he is aware of what is going on in our inmost minds; he can feel for us and sympathize with us. He is the fellow sufferer who loves and is loved. The vital difference between a human person and God is described by Hartshorne:

> . . . that whereas the character individual to a man cannot be stated in mere abstract terms, such as good or wise or perverse or foolish (all such characteristics being, for all that could be known, applicable to other individuals) God's character, on the contrary, can be described utterly in terms which yet are unique to him as the one divine individual. Only one individual can ever be omniscient, primordial and everlasting, all loving, supreme cause of all effects, and supreme

effect of all causes. Only one individual can ever be divine. Here is an extremely abstract character which yet is the defining characteristic of a self or a person. This character though individual to God, is so abstract and non specific that it can be correlated with every possible character you please in this correlate, the world.[24]

The proposal that God is a person raises the specter of anthropomorphism. Why not use the term "reality" instead of "God"? The fact is that in neo-classical theism the word "God" is more meaningful than the word "reality," because it endows the word with ultimate significance. In classical theism God is in actuality impersonal. Heschel suggests that the biblical idea of man made in the image of God points to a theomorphic anthropology rather than anthropomorphic. "Holy shall ye be, for I the Lord your God am holy."[25] The character of God as here described includes intelligence, valuation, and volition, which, Tenant says, "constitute the essence of personality as we know it in addition to the subjecthood it presupposes."[26]

A fourth proposition inherent in the world view derived from the New Science is the extended nature of man's freedom. Aristotle's view of the universe assigned to man the role of unfolding what had been enfolded by fate, nature, or God. The new *weltanschauung* imposes upon him the task of selecting goals as well as creating the means of attaining them. Men are free to decide among alternative ends and to find ways of realizing them. They are, thus, evaluating beings free to choose their course. This stress on radical freedom is integral not only to neo-classical theism, it is also a common factor among secularist philosophers, as shown by Sartre's assertion that man is condemned to be free, i.e., "every man without any support or help whatever, is condemned at every instance to invent man."[27] The fallacy of this view, as of secular humanism generally, is its failure to account for the order, growth, and unity of the totality of reality. To be sure, man is free to choose among alternatives, but he is guided by the experience of the whole, and the ONE. It has been suggested that causality is crystalized freedom, and freedom is causality in the making. Reality, then, is sheer action, and present creation adds its mite to the total organic data already accumulated. This places the responsibility for good and evil in the same species.

The problem of man's freedom and God's power is old. The talmudic sages suggested that "everything is in the power of heaven except the fear of heaven."[28] They recognized that a theism in which God is lawgiver and judge must of necessity endow man with the freedom to disobey him. Morality is impossible if man is not free to choose immorality. In the Middle Ages Jewish philosophers tended to limit man's freedom rather than lessen God's omnipotence. In classical theism, generally, God as creator limits himself by granting man the freedom to disregard the divine will and to suffer the consequences. Whitehead's metaphysics, which is the foundation of neo-classic theism, rules out the idea of God possessing any coercive power whatsoever. It dismisses *creatio ex nihilo*, proposing instead that God is not *before* all creation, he is, rather, *with* creation. In the traditional view, which attributes to God omnipotence, writes Whitehead, "the deepest idolatry, the fashioning of God in the image of the Egyptian, Persian, Roman imperial rulers, was retained. The church gave unto God the attributes which belonged exclusively to Caesar."[29] This the classical tradition has retained both in concept and language, still speaking of "Kings of Kings."

God's power is coercive in classical theism even though he grants man the freedom to rebel. This view is discredited by man's experience in history, since coercive power means control, and also the power to prevent innocent suffering. The Nazi holocaust cannot be explained by the assertion that in some disastrous events of history God hides his face for reasons beyond man's comprehension. Such a God, as Richard Rubenstein has described, is a monster. The idea of an omnipotent being possessing both coercive power and unlimited love is disabused in history. Beyond this wholly unacceptable view, Lewis Ford reminds us that "To the extent that God exercises such power, creaturely freedom is restricted, the reality of the world is diminished, and the divine experience is impoverished. Creaturely freedom is all important, for without it God is deprived of the one thing the world can provide which God alone cannot have; a genuine social existence."[30]

Power, however, need not be coercive, it can be persuasive and unlimited. God creates by persuading the world to create itself. This is effective only as men choose and confirm the purposes which are urged upon them. That there has been an evolutionary movement from the simple to the complex is undeniable. It is no more to be explained by chance than by coercive power. The existence of a power directing this process over billions of years, a power introducing richer possibilities of order for the world to actualize, is inescapable. "God proposes," says Ford, "and the world disposes." He goes on to say: "Any divine power which so influences the world without violating its integrity is properly called persuasive, which the necessary self-activity of the creature insures the spontaneity of response. This spontaneity may be minimal for protons and electrons, but in the course of the evolutionary advances, sustained until now, it has manifested itself in ever richer forms as the vitality of living cells, the conscious activity of the higher animals, and the selfconscious freedom of man. *Spontaneity has matured as freedom*. On this level it becomes possible for the increasing complexity of order to be directed toward the achievement of civilization, and for the means of divine persuasion to become ethical aspiration. The devout will affirm that in the ideals we envision we are being persuaded by God, but this self-conscious awareness is not necessary for its effectiveness. Not only we ourselves, but the entire created order, whether consciously or unconsciously, is open to this divine persuasion, each in its own way."[31]

It follows from this view that tragedy is an inseparable ingredient of freedom which, along with chance, is bound together with law and design. The root of tragedy lies in free activity, since creatures can choose not to be persuaded. All free creatures are more or less dangerous, and the most free is man. Born to freedom, man is born to tragedy; but he is also born to opportunity. The role of God, the supreme creativity, is to inspire lesser creative action, and to take it up into his own unsurpassable actuality. In this process opportunities for existence outweigh its risks, and life becomes essentially good. In a poetic passage toward the end of *Process and Reality* Whitehead writes:

> The wisdom of subjective aim prehends every actuality for what it can be in such a perfect system—its sufferings, its sorrows, its failures, its triumphs, its immediacies of joy—woven by rightness of feeling into

the harmony of universal feeling, which is always immediate, always
with novel advance, moving onward and never perishing. The revolts
of destructive evil, purely self-regarding, are dismissed into their
triviality of merely individual facts; and yet the good they did achieve
in individual joy, in individual sorrow, in the introduction of needed
contrast, is yet saved by its relation to the completed whole. The
image—and it is but an image—the image under which this operative
growth of God's nature is best conceived is that of a tender care that
nothing is lost.

The consequent nature of God is his judgment on the world. He
saves the world as it passes into the immediacy of his own life. It is the
judgment of a tenderness which loses nothing that can be saved. It is
also the judgment of a wisdom which uses what in the temporal world
is mere wreckage.[32]

Freed from the theological framework of the biblical age the
primary interest of the prophetic faith is God's concern for man. The
power of God to coerce his will is ever-present, but his persistent
effort is to persuade men to do good and not evil. That men do not
heed his pleading but disregard it awakens in him a profound feeling
of pathos. Heschel has described God's involvement with the world:
"To the prophets the relationship of the world to the transcendent is
signified by the participation of God (pathos) in the world. Not
self-sufficiency, but concern and involvement characterize His relation to the world."[33] He is never presented as a metaphysical entity
beyond change. "At one moment I may decree that a nation or a
kingdom shall be uprooted and pulled down and destroyed; but if
that nation against which I made the decree turns back from its
wickedness, I change My mind concerning the punishment I
planned to bring on it."[34]

The reality of God is sensed in pathos rather than in power. It is
more like the pity that we feel for people who have eyes, see not,
and having ears, hear not. Heschel says that "God's repenting a
decision which was based on moral grounds clearly shows the su-
premacy of pathos. . . . Divine ethos does not operate without
pathos. . . . His ethos and pathos are one. . . . Since the prophets
do not speak in the name of the moral law, it is inaccurate to
characterize them as proclaimers of justice, or *mishpat*. It is more

accurate to see them as proclaimers of God's pathos, speaking not for the idea of justice, but for the God of justice, for God's concern for justice. . . . Pathos, concern for the world, is the very ethos of God."[35] No word of God is the final word; his judgments are conditional. A change in man's response brings about a change in God's judgment. "Love is the ultimate principle of justice," wrote Tillich, "love reunites, justice preserves what is to be united. It is the form in which love performs its work. Justice in its ultimate meaning is the creative justice, and creative justice is the form of reuniting love."[36] The prophets sought the reunion of the separate parts which neo-classical theism defines as God's primary goal. He is an ultimate source of values in an ongoing, dynamic activity.

Western civilization today is not in harmony with the basic character of the universe as post-modern science describes it. Materialism dominates our culture at the very time when the universe is disclosed to be non-material. Fragmentation is increasingly the mode of human organization, as the universe is described as an integrative unity; fierce competition among men and nations, when the universe is described as relational, whole, and one. Rugged individualism is extolled as a high virtue in a universe which emphasizes individuality in community. The major drive in Western culture aims at separating the part from the whole. In addition to these disharmonies there is persuasive evidence that man himself is being transformed into a machine at the very time when the universe reflects qualities of personhood. The rise of technology in the service of sophisticated science is threatening the very existence of all life on earth. Nature is described as organic while man increasingly behaves as a mechanism. The brutality of the Nazis fell far below the savagery of the wildest animal. Only a man turned into a mechanism can plan and operate an Auschwitz. In this moment of history man possesses the power to destroy the unity of the planet, and ultimately the planet itself.

The paradox that baffles modern man is that he finds himself in a life-and-death struggle at the very hour that his secular endeavors have succeeded so brilliantly. The evils which threatened human existence in the past—hunger, disease, natural calamities—are in increasing measure today subject to control and even disappearance. The advances made through increased use of science and reason are truly wonderful, and to an earlier generation would have been called miracles. The tragic irony lies in the fact that the very instrument which holds the promise of man's liberation—scientific technology—has itself become the source of the possible, some believe the probable, end of life on earth. Prophecies of doom are proclaimed today not in the name of God, but by Nobel Prize–winning scientists, social scientists, and, as we have seen, sensitive creative artists. All of this is happening as one *weltanschauung* is fading and another is taking its place—theism is giving way to secularism. What men believe about the universe and their place in it sooner or later determines what they do.

Secular humanists today feed upon the moral heritage which was an integral part of a theistic *weltanschauung*. Even though they reject that world view, they formally applaud the virtue of self-sacrifice on behalf of a greater and distant good. Tomorrow, their sons, facing the complex and perplexing issues of their day, will still call upon reason and good will to resolve them. The culture in which they will make their moral decisions will be secularistic, which will reduce the virtue of self-sacrifice to a senseless whim in a world itself absurd. Their grandchildren, confronted with colossal crises, social and physical, which will call for abundant self-sacrifice, will be faced with Toulmin's limiting question: "Why should I be moral at all?" Walter Lippmann in the twenties recognized the dilemma of the secular view of life. "Each ideal," he wrote, "is supreme within a sphere of its own. There is no point of reference outside of which he can determine the relative value of competing ideals. . . . his impulses are no longer part of one attitude toward life, his ideals are no longer in one hierarchy under one lordly ideal."[37] The Norse myth describing the twilight of the gods, the *Gotterdammerung*, seems to be upon us. The legend also foretells the setting of the sun upon man and the beginning of an eternity during which the world, untenanted by deity and humanity alike, will endure in formless void. The present prospect of human extinction through nuclear war, exhaustion of resources, pollution of air, water, and earth, is a real and frightening concern of thoughtful people today. Concurrently, the

God-faith is rapidly declining. Has the myth of *Gotterdammerung* turned into reality for modern man?

Tradition has preserved the prophetic faith in its classical theological form. It is, however, readily appropriated by the new cultural climate of the postmodern world. In fact, freed from its Biblical theological formulation, it takes on enriched meaning, as was suggested above, and becomes important in our search for a faith adequate to the present human condition. Walter Kaufmann, a secular humanist, commenting upon Isaiah's prophecy "In the days to come . . . they shall beat their swords into plowshares, and their spears into pruning hooks,"[38] writes:

> It is hard to do justice to the originality of men who in the eighth century B.C. untutored by the horrors of two world wars with poison gas and atomic bombs, and without the frightening prospect of still more fearful weapons of destruction, insisted that war is evil and must some day be abolished, and that all peoples must someday learn to dwell together in peace. In retrospect we may say that they spelled out explicitly what was implicit in the Old Testament conception of God and man. There is nothing wrong with putting it that way, provided we remember how long it has taken the mass of men to perceive the very same implication.[39]

Like most authentic secularists, Kaufmann enthusiastically accepts the ethical vision of the prophets, but warns us against entangling it in a theological frame which encumbers it with irrelevancy. Historically the moral vision of the prophets got lost in a tangled skein of religiosity. They were theists who began by asking: "And what the Lord requires of you: Only to do justice, and to love goodness, and to walk modestly with your God."[40] The prophets were not preachers of religiosity, their emphasis was upon morality not feelings. Recently the United States Supreme Court ruled that the claim of a conscientious objector to war on religious grounds is valid even if he denies the existence of a supreme being.[41] The Court in this decision legitimizes the idea that secular humanism qualifies for the designation of religion. Modern culture views the postulate of God as unnecessary, and at times even an embarrassment. If the

Hebrew prophet were to visit our world today he would not be at home in the company of the religious, nor in that of the secular humanists. The first would find his demands for justice too radical, the second would not be interested in what God requires of them. Modern culture is fundamentally inhospitable to the prophetic faith in ethical monotheism.

Messianic futurism is a basic doctrine of the prophetic view of history, which for them is coherent, morally conditioned, and purposive—it is not a succession of events devoid of an ultimate goal. Indeed, the purpose of human existence is to help move history toward that end which was planned from the beginning. "I foretell the end from the beginning, and from the start, things that had not occurred. I say: My plan shall be fulfilled; I will do all that I have purposed."[42] In his charming book *The World of Our Fathers*, Irving Howe speaks of "that great Jewish mania—the future." The prophets reached out beyond the immediate critical events of their own nation toward a future goal of universal history. Unlike Plato, whose ethical concern was limited to philosophers and to the boundaries of Greece, the prophets extended their vision to all of humanity. They were not starry-eyed idealists untutored in the realities of the human condition. When Isaiah accepted the call to prophecy, he knew before he began that the people would not listen to him and would experience terrible disaster.[43] Pessimism was an ingredient of the prophetic faith. "Can the Ethiopian change his skin, or the leopard his spots? Just as much can you do good, who are practiced in doing evil."[44]

One wonders at the persistence of the prophets in the face of their acknowledged hopelessness. In the main they were not apocalyptists depending upon divine intervention when all else failed. Basically, they believed that the people must be persuaded to do good and to avoid evil. Their hope that the people would be persuaded was very dim. Hope was a frail reed to lean upon in the short range; faith in God, however, was compelling in the long range. Isaiah looked forward to a saving remnant, Deutero-Isaiah to new things coming, and Jeremiah to a new heart. In the prophetic view men are free to disregard God's pleadings, to their own hurt, and to his suffering and pathos. God as creator cannot be defeated in his ultimate purpose. "In the days to come . . . they shall beat their swords into plowshares, and their spears to pruning hooks; nation shall not take up sword against nation; they shall never again know war."[45] Rabbi Tarphon wrote this prophetic faith into the Rabbinic tradition: "It is not incumbent upon you to complete the job, but you are not free to desist from it altogether."[46]

Jeremiah more cogently than any prophet understood God as both judge and redeemer.

> Just as I was watchful over them to uproot and to pull down, to overthrow and to destroy, and to bring disaster, so will I be watchful over them to build and to plant. . . . See a time is coming—declares the Lord—when I will make a new covenant with the House of Israel and the House of Judah. . . . But such is the covenant I will make with the House of Israel after these days—declares the Lord: I will put My Teaching into their inmost being and inscribe it upon their hearts. Then I will be their God, and they shall be My people. No longer will they need to teach one another and say to one another, "Heed the Lord," for all of them from the least to the greatest shall heed Me—declares the Lord.[47]

Confidence in the ultimate fulfillment of God's purpose as creator was the hallmark of prophetic faith.

This teleological view of history characterized human culture in its classical theological formulation until Darwin's time. There were variations on the theme. Judaism and Christianity differed on the nature of the final goal. In the nineteenth century naturalists discerned a design in nature which pointed to an intelligent designer. The order pervading the inorganic and organic, as well as human reason could be explained by a "good purposer." In the previous century Paley's famous metaphor of the watch and the watchmaker became the picturesque slogan for the belief in God the creator of all that exists. "In every nature and every portion of nature which we can descry, we find attention bestowed even upon the minutest parts. The hinges in the wings of an earwig and the joints of its tennae, are as highly wrought as if the creator had nothing else to finish. We see no signs of diminution of care by multiplicity of objects, or distraction of thought by variety."[48] The Hebrew prophets were not professional naturalists, yet they would have felt at home in Paley's view of nature, man, and God the intelligent designer.

The publication of Darwin's *Origin of Species* effectively challenged Paley's man-centered romantic evolutionism, as well as his notion of the watch and the watchmaker. Eisley describes the confrontation in positive language: "Darwin had delivered a death blow to a naively simple form of design argument, but Huxley himself came to realize it is still possible to argue for directivity in the process of life, even though that directivity may be without finality in the human sense."[49] Darwin believed that "it is derogatory that the creator of countless systems of worlds should have created each of the myriads of creeping parasites and slimy worms which have swarmed each day of life . . . on this globe."[50] Special creation implied the creation of a plant or animal or human for a fixed purpose for all time, a final design, and a creator who made each of the creations in its final form. Darwin's work refuted this theory of special creation and introduced instead the concept of evolution through a struggle for existence, natural selection, and chance variations. It did not, however, reject the existence of a creator, only one who creates every separate thing or creature. Nature makes things make themselves; there is no need for a master-craftsman.

Philosophers later argued that the *Origin of Species* is invalid unless one postulates a creative being teleologically directing the process of evolution. Tenant, for example, concedes that evolution from the amoeba to man can be explained by non-teleological causation only if we grant self-preservation as the law of life. But, he goes on to say: "it is rather when the essential part played by the environment, physical and organic, in the progressive development of the organic world is appreciated, that non-teleological explanation ceases to be plausible in this sphere, and conspiration being precluded, external design begins to be indicated, or strongly suggested."[51] He rejects the theory of unconscious purpose, saying: "If nature evinces wisdom, the wisdom is another's."[52] There is a *good* toward which progress aims;

> [The moral data] enable us to advance from belief that the world is a work of art to belief that it is constructed for a purpose, and worthily

specifies what the purpose is, or includes. If we decline to explain things thus, it would seem that the only alternative is to regard the self-subsistent entities, of which the world is constituted, as comparable with the letters of type which shuffled themselves not only into a book or a literature, but also into a reader commanding the particular tongue in which the book utters its unintentional meaning. If evidence from cumulative adaptiveness to design be non-logical, as is admitted, it at least is not unreasonable.[53]

Commenting on Tenant's view Peter Bertocci writes: "The world's *thusness* cannot be explained, therefore, apart from a creative Being, who purposed the realization of moral values, beyond whom we need not and cannot go, but to whom we *must* go if a sufficient reason is to be given for cosmic evolution. . . . Man as creature possessed of the power to think offers the best known clue to the nature of that purpose . . . on man and his values. Tenant completes the curve begun by plotting the relationship between the inorganic world of law and an organic world driven by self-preservation."[54] The empirical philosopher, in this case, argues that the order and arrangement of the universe cannot be explained adequately without reference to the activity of an intelligent, teleological God.

Whitehead asked why the trend of evolution has been upwards. "The fact that organic species have been produced from inorganic distributions of matter, and the fact that in the lapse of time organic species of higher and higher types have evolved are not in the least explained by any doctrine of adaptation to the environment, or of struggle."[55] He finds the answer in the fact that lower forms of creatures adapt themselves to the environment, while the higher forms of life are actively engaged in modifying their environment. The most prominent fact in man's existence is his active engagement in modifying his environment, which is the primary function of his ability to reason. "This conclusion amounts to the thesis that Reason is a factor in experience which directs and criticizes the urge towards the attainment of an end realized in imagination but not in fact."[56] Man, the rational creature, is the latest, and in his complexity the highest, product of the evolutionary process. This exhibits an advance of increasing complexity of order over the past several billion years. It is possible, and the past testifies to it, that man will give way to an entirely different species of greater complexity, whether on earth or on some other planetary system. The past is always prologue in a universe that is essentially creative.

Neither chance, which the secularists propose as the explanation for the evolutionary advance from simple to complex, nor divine determinism, which classical theology, in its extreme form, gives as the real cause, is reasonable, because both omit the creative element. Only a power that introduces novel and higher possibilities for nature and for man to accept and to actualize makes sense. Lewis Ford's succinct statement has been quoted above, "God proposes and the world disposes."[57] God tries to persuade, the world either accepts or rejects. God's aim and purpose is unique in that "he always aims at a maximum total of intensity of satisfaction for all concerned. . . . [In human terms] God never lazily aims at second best, nor is he ever selfish or self-centered."[58] The proton and the neutron give minimal response, but, in the course of evolutionary advance, living cells lead to higher animals, and then to the self-conscious freedom of man. "Spontaneity has matured as freedom, the self-conscious awareness is not necessary to its effectiveness. Not only we ourselves, but the entire created order, whether consciously or unconsciously, is open to this divine persuasion, each in its own way."[59]

God, the fulfillment of whose purpose depends upon persuading the world to create itself, runs the risk of failure. Man, the most free of all creatures, is the most difficult to persuade. Intense in his feelings, God also *prehends* everything in the universe, so that man's actions and influence live everlastingly in him. All that man does affects God in his consequent nature, and thus affects the nature and destiny of the world. That man will not be persuaded to choose the good is an ever-present possibility, which history demonstrates to be the more probable eventuality. At this point, faith is the determining factor, faith in God whose reality lies in "our eradicable confidence in the final worth of existence. It lies in the nature of this basic confidence to affirm that the real whole of which we experience ourselves to be parts is such as to be worthy, and thus itself to evoke, that very confidence."[60] This faith is supported by the slow development in a very long history which moved from the simple amoeba to the complex nature of rational man. It is a faith that bears a short-range pessimism and a long-range optimism. Primarily, it is faith in the possibility that God as persuader will move men to actualize the novel opportunities he presents to advance history toward the divine goal. Speaking as a revolutionary atheistic humanist, Ernest Bloch points out that "Moses did not proclaim God in Canaan, but Canaan in God."[61] Instead of locating God in a settled land, the author of Exodus relates a land of promise to a God leading the way.

One of the most concise expressions of neo-classical theology which is acceptable in our postmodern culture was written by Schubert Ogden:

> . . . secularity tends by its own inner dynamism towards explicit faith in God. To affirm the significance and autonomy of this world, and to insist upon the rights and responsibility of human experience and reason, is to speak out of an underlying confidence in the worth of life that theistic belief alone can make fully explicit. This assumes, of course, that one can, and indeed must distinguish between theism as such, and classical theism of our philosophical-theological tradition with its gratuitous negations. But, if by theism one means the positive affirmation of the reality of God, of the irreducibility of religion, and of a truth about existence beyond the truth of science, it seems to me the only way to a secularity that is fully conscious, in that it grasps reflectively and explicably the basic faith in the worth of life that it itself implies.[62]

The prophetic faith, freed from the classical theological frame, is not only acceptable to our postmodern culture, it is enriched and becomes more significant. Ethical monotheism takes on importance in a universe which is basically one, wholly rational, and purposive. God, the untiring persuader and prehender, lies at the very heart of the prophetic message. There is, however, a very important difference between the neo-classical theologian and the spokesmen for the prophetic faith. Philosophers and theologians explain the world, the prophets were men dedicated to changing the world. In the next and final chapter we will examine the relevance of the prophetic faith to the human condition today.

Chapter 5

Creation and Liberation

Theology should be distinguished from both faith and religious experience. It is a by-product of these and is arrived at by reflection and rational examination. Basically, it abstracts from living religions those experiences which are reducible to a self-conscious system. It is, usually, an enterprise for the professional religionist; in a broad sense, everyone theologizes whether he knows it or not. Theology should especially be distinguished from philosophy, whose role is cognitive, examining reality as such. Philosophy deals with structures, categories, and concepts expressed in general terms and abstracts. It aims at universal free inquiry, pursuing knowledge for its own sake. Theology differs from philosophy in that it is specific and concrete, dealing with one particular system of faith. Tillich properly denies the possibility of Christian philosophy but affirms the legitimacy of Christian theology. A theologian is a thinker whose roots are in a historical tradition, or who deliberately puts himself within it by an act of faith.

Two strains of thought run through Western civilization which significantly affected the character of its theological enterprise, Greek philosophy and Hebrew religion. The first is essentially static and contemplative, the second derives from action. James Barr says that "Movement could not be ultimate reality for the Greeks to whom being must be distinguished from becoming, and the ultimate must be changeless. For the Israelites, the true reality was action and movement, and the inactive and motionless was no reality at all."[1] The dynamic manifests itself in the Hebrew concern with history; God acts in history and is the sum of his acts. Moses does not see God, he sees the connection between slavery and his own life. The Book of Chronicles offers a theological interpretation of Israel's past history, and the Book of Deuteronomy does the same thing. Past events are recalled in order to discover their meaning. The prophets announced *truth* as they received it in a historical situation and then called upon the people to act and fulfill it. They were neither theologians nor philosophers; they were witnesses for the word to be put in praxis.

The Greek view of history is naturalistic, it moves in recurring cycles which are governed by prescribed laws. God remains transcendent vis-à-vis the individual and the process of coming to be and passing away. Aristotle does not interpret the history of a people, since mankind is not dependent upon historical happenings. Events reveal themselves so that nothing ever happened once and for all. The Hebrews, however, note categories of decision, human responsibility, and man's eternal relationship to the future. Human existence is determined by the historical situation and the decisions that interpreted it. It is not determined by some unalterable substance or preprogrammed character. Fundamentally the distinction is between the abstract and the concrete. Hebrew thought dealt less with abstractions than with actual objects and situations. There is also a sharp contrast between them in their conception of the nature of man. The Greek view maintains a duality: the soul is imprisoned in a material body. In the Hebrew view the soul and flesh are not separable. "The conflict between the individual and the collectivity arises from the Greek tradition," says Barr, "but for the Hebrew life was lived in a social totality of religion and justice."[2]

Liberation theology, the latest arrival on the theological scene, expresses a vigorous protest against the abstractions of classical (Greek) religious thought. The oppressed people of the world yearn for the God who revealed himself in the *act* of liberating an enslaved people from Egyptian bondage. "Only the white middle class," writes Herzog, "or the affluent can afford to start with the self in the search for the meaning of God. . . . The more self-certainty that could be had, the less God certainty was necessary. One needs leisure and privacy to find self-certainty."[3] He goes on to say that God is a live issue only where life is not secure, where man cannot become complacent, and when he realizes he is not in control of his own life. Modern mainstream theology begins either with Cartesian philosophy and a self whose mind is free of all care, and assured of untroubled leisure and peaceful solitude, or with Kierkegaardian existentialism and a self isolated from the living world. Most of the people of the world do not live in so rarefied an atmosphere. Liberation theology is rooted in Hebrew thought, which, as we have seen, seeks to know the meaning of God in the dynamic, often eruptive, events of history. Richard Niebuhr denies the possibility of disinterested theology: "Whatever be the case in other human inquiries, there is no such thing as disinterested theology, since no one can speak of God or gods at all save as valued beings or as values which cannot be apprehended save by a willing, feeling, responding self."[4] James Cone, in a similar spirit, argues that "theology is not a universal language; it is rather an interested language, reflecting the goals and aspirations of a particular people in a definite social setting."[5]

The major thrust of mainstream theology today aims at meeting the growing challenge of a secular world, of man come of age. It glistens with the patina of Academe, reflecting the culture of the middle class. "[T]he problem of Western academic theology in America," writes Van Harvey, "and the West generally, is that it cannot break out of the horizon of the bourgeois world and bring a transcendent word of judgment and renewal to the conditions that create the 'life worlds' of Western men and women."[6] The vast majority of religious people are not disturbed by ontological or cosmological doubts, because they are neither professional theologians nor philosophers. The serious challenge which faces the modern theologian comes "from the man who is not a man, who is not recognized as such by the existing social order; he is in the ranks of the poor, the exploited; he is the man who is systematically despoiled of his being as a man. . . . the question, therefore is not how to speak of God in an adult world, but how to proclaim Him as a Father in a world that is not human."[7]

This is the only theological problem confronting the people of the third world today. It is also the source of the impatience of black theologians in America with the bourgeois (white) theologians who enjoy the leisure to speculate philosophically. Neither the third-world man nor the black man is an unbeliever. He just does not know the answer to the question, *Am I a man?* Women, historically the oldest oppressed people, face what Mary Daly describes as a "world wide phenomenon of a sexual caste system, the same whether one lives in Saudi Arabia or Sweden. This planetary caste system involves birth ascribed hierarchically ordered groups whose members have unequal access to goods, services, prestige, and to physical and mental well being."[8]

Among the disinherited of the earth is the modern Jew, who is imprisoned in a demonic slave camp called anti-Semitism from which there appears to be no deliverance. Saul Bellow, reflecting on his recent visit to the State of Israel, writes: "Under Hitler Jews were lepers of Europe. No, they were worse than lepers. Lepers are isolated, nursed, treated. There is no word for what the Jews were in Europe between 1939–1945. After the war the survivors fled Europe. They were not welcome in other countries. They went to Palestine—to Israel."[9] Creative artists, as was suggested in our first chapter, are often reliable prophets. Bellow, as both artist and Jew, projects a thought that crosses the minds of many modern Jews: "Wouldn't it be the most horrible of ironies if the Jews had collected themselves conveniently in one country for a second Holocaust. . . . you cannot take your right to live for granted. Others can. You cannot. This is not to say that everyone else is living pleasantly and well under a decent regime. No, it means only that the Jews, because they are Jews, have never been able to take the right to live as a natural right."[10]

More than half of the peoples of the world, cutting across racial, sexual, ethnic, national, and religious lines, are imprisoned in oppressive and unrelenting poverty which tortures the body and depresses the soul. Every year more than a half-million of them die of hunger. What is their relationship to God the Father if their misery and death are of no more importance than the extinction of cockroaches? Mainstream theology ignores their groaning, being fixed in its own bourgeois entrapment. Each oppressed community tends to view its insufferable condition in isolation, unaware of demons enslaving other groups all over the world. Two bonds should unite them—a common need for liberation, and a sense of the historical process that envelops all of them. Though sinned against, none is without sin. The danger lies in the desire for separation which each oppressed group favors, and in the more serious practice of casting the blame upon another oppressed community, charging it as the oppressor. "It remains to be seen," says Rosemary Ruether, "how willing Liberation theologians will be to cooperate with this massacre of others, and ultimately of themselves. . . . only together does this enlargement of the boundaries of the world and of *God* cease to be fashionable verbiage, and become a concrete stake in changing the world."[11] It is evident that theology can no longer escape the urgent issues which the life-worlds of modern men and women who must act and seek justice demand.

Liberation theology has its roots in the prophetic tradition. Both are basically existential as against metaphysical speculation. Neither of them speaks the language of the philosopher's abstractions, but only that which describes a particular historical situation in which the divine is either involved or experienced. The prophets, as we have suggested, were not theologians, they did not reflect on the question of God's being in himself. Their primary concern was the meaning of God in a contemporary event. Those who today speak for the liberation of the oppressed of the world are not performing the work of the theologians. Like the prophets, they are witnesses to a faith already established, but are not engaged in a critical examination of the truth or reality of that faith. In a previous chapter we proposed that the prophetic faith must be freed from the classical theological formulation if it is to speak meaningfully to the postmodern age and make clear what it means to speak of God in a day when secularism is becoming the dominant culture. Is God omnipotent, wholly transcendent, and beyond change? The liberation theologies now current contain almost nothing which can be classified as theology; i.e., a meaningful doctrine of God which is intellectually adequate for minds fashioned by science and critical rationalism. Their criticism of the mainline theologians for their neglect of the theological problems which arise from the life-worlds is both war-ranted and challenging. Theology today cannot afford to disregard either the challenge of modern secularism or the demands of the oppressed for liberation in a universe in which God is both Creator and Liberator.

The separation between faith and works was debated in the early church. Paul's assertion that "a man is justified by faith without deeds of the law"[12] was apparently contradicted in the Letter of James: "For as a body without the spirit is dead, so faith without works is dead also."[13] Modern New Testament scholars question the assertion that James was correcting Paul. That, however, is not pertinent to our concern here except as it bears upon the protest of liberation theologians against mainline theologians for their neglect of works which faith demands. The confusion here arises from the misuse of the word "theology" to describe the present religious-lib-eration movement. Theology is *logos*, thought about God, which is, with very few exceptions, wholly disregarded by those who speak for liberation theology today. Their case is weakened by their failure to reexamine the theological frame in which their religious claim for human liberation is made, making it irrelevant to the secularistic challenge to the reality of God's existence.

The prophetic tradition is not entirely free of the separate claims of faith, which is *believing*, and works, which is *doing*. Isaiah chastised those who relied on doing: "Ha! Those who go down to Egypt for help and rely upon horses! They have put their trust in abundance of chariots, in vast numbers of riders, and they have not turned to the Holy One of Israel, they have not sought the Lord."[14] One could conclude from this passage, and several others, that the prophet was preaching a program of faith without works, putting his trust in believing without doing. Such a conclusion, however, misses the meaning of faith as the prophet understood it. The Hebrew word for "faith," *emunah*, is usually associated with *tsedek*, "righteousness," and is virtually a synonym for "justice," "truth," and "honesty." Sheldon Blank writes: "A word may be known by the company it keeps. One way to understand the Hebrew word for faith, *Emunah*, is through acquaintance with its associates."[15] "And I will espouse you forever: I will espouse you with righteousness and justice, and with goodness and mercy, and I will espouse you with [*emunah*] faithfulness; then you shall be devoted to the Lord."[16] Habakkuk proclaimed the inseparability of faith and deed: "*Tsadik b'emunoto yihye* [The righteous shall live by his faith]."[17] One of the revealing uses of *emunah* is in Isaiah: "*Im lo taaminu ki lo tayomaynu* [If you have no faith, you shall not endure]."[18] The prophets conceived of believing and doing as one act, and thus avoided the confusion which the early church experienced, and which remains a serious deficiency in modern religious thought.

The prophetic faith rests upon the theological foundation which declares that God liberates as he creates. The tradition says: "When God began to create the heaven and the earth,—and the earth being *tohu v'vohu*, unformed and void."[19] The prophets were not concerned with the problems involved with *creatio ex nihilo*, what was there before creation? They understood creation as the prelude to the process of actualization which moves toward the divine goals. In that process God is both Liberator and Creator, bringing order out of the chaos in which it all began. His liberation of Israel from Egyptian slavery was to be climaxed with the acceptance of Yahweh, Israel's God, as the one and only God of all the peoples of the earth. Deutero-Isaiah, speaking in the Babylonian exile, announced the vision of a new exodus. Creation is a continuous process of liberation in which God and man move toward the end of days when universal justice and peace will be realized. God's role is to set before man new opportunities which he is free to accept or reject. "As of now, I announce to you new things, well-guarded secrets you did not know. Only now are they created, and not of old; before today you had not heard them; you cannot say, 'I knew them already.' "[20]

The Jewish tradition has preserved in its liturgy the prophetic view of God as Creator-Liberator. Each day the Jew prays: "In his [God's] goodness, he renews daily the work of creation." In the Kiddush, the sanctification prayer recited over the wine at the beginning of the Sabbath: *Zikoron l'maasay b'reshit*—"in remembrance of the act of creation"; this is followed with *Zayher l'tsiat mitsrayim*—"a memorial to the exodus from Egypt." The Jew is constantly reminded that the reason for his existence as a Jew lies in his positive response to God's call for his help in the divine work of creation and liberation.

There are aspects of life which are not satisfied, seemingly, by this prophetic definition of the relationship between God and man. Man's fate and destiny as an individual is, as Hermann Cohen reminded us, an unnecessary question. "A Jew does not ask what is my fate? What is my destiny? He asks only, what is my duty?"[21] This is the prophetic view of the meaning of human existence. Nevertheless, human life is by nature transient and ends in death. There was a time when it did not exist, and there will be a time when it will not exist. The Atonement Day liturgy describes the transient nature of human life: "Man is but flesh and blood, his origin dust, his end dust. He wears out his life for his daily bread; he is like the grass that withereth, the flower that fadeth, like a shadow that moveth on, like a cloud that passeth by, like a mote of dust driven by the wind, a dream that is forgotten."[22] The transiency and meaninglessness of human existence, which is also expressed in Psalm 90, appeals to God as redeemer and savior. The last line of the Atonement prayer responds with the declaration: "But thou art the Eternal King, the ever living God." Man is a transient being "like a dream that is forgotten." That is his nature. Only God is *eternal* and ever *living*, not man. The psalmist appeals to God for redemption: "Establish thou also upon us the work of our hands; yea, the work of our hands establish thou it."[23] In either case it is God who gives meaning to what is meaningless without him.

Man, being free, may choose to sin; i.e., to reject what God proposes. The Hebrew word *ḥayt* means straying from the path which God has set for man to follow. There is no redemption for him unless he returns to that path. "Return, O Israel, to the Lord your God, for you have fallen because of your sin."[24] Man, being human, sins, strays from the path, but he is free to return to it until the day he dies. He is born neither a sinner nor a saint; he is born with two tendencies—one to do good, the other to do evil, and being free he must choose. God cannot save him or redeem him from sin unless he freely chooses to do what God has purposed for him. "The more the prophetic conception of the moral nature of the Deity permeated the Jewish religion," wrote Kaufmann Kohler, "the more the term sin came to mean an offense against the holiness of God, the Guardian of morality. Hence, the great prophets upbraided the people for their morals, not their ceremonial failings."[25] The prophets did not separate the role of God as Creator-Liberator into redemption, salvation, and emancipation. The problems raised by transiency, death, and sin find their answer in man's fulfillment of his role of co-worker with God in the ultimate achievement of the kingdom of God on earth.

Jean-Jacques Rousseau believed that man is born free yet is held in chains everywhere. The biblical account of the history of Israel demonstrates that what the French philosopher observed to be the condition of man in the eighteenth century was true in ancient days. Israel was set free from bondage only to learn that it was just the first step in a long process which was marked by a constant struggle with little success, much failure, and a constant renewal. Freedom is never a permanent possession achieved once and for all. Threatening forces arise from without and from within. The generation that was set free from Egyptian slavery wandered forty years in the wilderness only to become eager to return to bondage rather than suffer the hardships which the march toward the promised land demanded. The experience of those forty miserable years became a paradigm for the message of the Hebrew prophets. Once Israel entered Canaan it turned out to be a land of unrelieved warfare against foreign nations, a land in which the kings of Israel were often oppressive of their own people, a kingdom in which the rich wallowed in luxury at the expense of the poor. The prophet roared against this breach of Israel's covenant with God. "Hear this word, you cows of Bashan on the hill of Samaria—who defraud the poor, who rob the needy, who say to your husbands, 'Bring and let's carouse.' "[26] This prophetic protest is echoed in the New Testament:

> . . . a word to you who have great possessions. Weep and wail over the miserable fate descending on you. Your riches have rotted; your fine clothes are moth-eaten; your silver and gold have rusted away, and their very rust will be evidence against you and consume your flesh like fire. You have piled up wealth in an age that is very near its close. The wages you never paid to the men who mowed your fields are loud

against you, and the outcry of the reapers has reached the Lord. You
have lived on earth in wanton luxury, fattening yourselves like cat-
tle—and the day of the slaughter has come. You have condemned the
innocent and murdered him; he offers no resistance.[27]

The prophets warned against all attempts to sunder liberation
from creation. Freedom endows man with the obligation to choose
to be persuaded by God's call to him to become his co-worker in the
making of a future which will be better than the past or the present,
or to choose not to be persuaded. Freedom is possible only when
men accept their place in the whole, the ONE, and their responsibility for the well-being of all others and their freedom to live
authentic selves. Each person is a unity, a one, even as the world is
one. The human body is not the source of evil, nor is the soul the
source of good. Adam is not tragically enslaved, he is tragically
tempted because he is human and free. Liberation cannot be sev-
ered from the responsibility of freedom of choice in the moral realm.
God's freedom is limited by man's freedom, and the fulfillment of
the work of creation is dependent upon man's faithful cooperation.
    The world is unfinished, always in the process of becoming. A
picture of the final goal is both unnecessary and impossible. In fact
Whitehead's view that process is reality is probably the best that we
can do with a definition of the final state of the future. "Things can be
otherwise," writes Ernest Bloch, "that means that things can also
become otherwise; in the direction of evil which must be avoided, or
in the direction of good which would have to be promoted."[28] It is
true that men are made for freedom, as Rousseau said, but the vast
majority of them do not possess it. Liberation, then, is modern
man's primary need, as it was at the beginning. Today, he needs
liberation from oppressive poverty, from political and social domination, and from structured and systematic denial of human rights.
Man as man needs the freedom to live in responsible authenticity as
a person. Liberation calls for a better understanding of history, of
which Gutierrez writes:

A conscientization of a tragic historical situation and the human
being's responsibility for a better destiny. . . . to conceive history as a

process of liberation of man is to consider freedom as a spiritual
conquest; it is to understand that the step from the abstract to a real
freedom is not taken without struggle against all the forces that
oppress man, a struggle full of pitfalls, detours, and temptations to run
away. The goal is not only better living conditions, a radical change of
structure, a special revolution; it is much more a continuous creation,
never ending, a new way to be a man, a permanent cultural revolution.[29]

In a profound sense liberation is what the whole world is all about, it
is a *mitzvah*, a covenantal demand.

The French Revolution heralded the secular version of the prophetic view of history. Social progress, guided by reason, was
moving humanity toward Liberty, Equality, and Fraternity. The
kingdom of God was being realized without transcendent judgment,
and without divine participation. The debacle of this secular hope is
today a matter of record. More than half of the people in the world
live in dehumanizing poverty, and more than three quarters of the
people in the world suffer various degrees of misery because they
are black, female, Jews, or victims of colonialism. The Gulag Archi-
pelago is not new to Brazil, Uruguay, or Chile. Gunnar Myrdal
estimates that U.S. corporations directly or indirectly control or
decisively influence between 70 percent and 90 percent of the raw
materials of Latin America, and probably half of its banking, indus-
try, commerce, and foreign trade. "Men are castrated by a social
system," writes Mary Daly, "in which destructive competitiveness
treats men who are low on the totem pole (e.g. Black males, poor
males, non-competitive males, Third world males, etc.) like
women. Yet all of these can look down upon primordially castrated
beings—women; these primordial eunuchs are rising to castrate not
people, but the *system* that castrates—that Great Father of us all
which indulges senselessly and universally in the politics of rape."[30]

We are witnessing an increasing trend toward revolutionary
action in the world today aimed at changing the basic economic and
political structure in the hope that it will improve the miserable
conditions in which masses of people are living. More than a third of
the people of the world are living in Communist countries although
very few of them are theoretical Marxists. They just have done what

must be done, as was the case in Cuba and China. "There is no way for the poor countries to develop adequately unless the rich countries reduce the huge proportion they contribute to the total impact. This involves a programme of de-development of the rich world. The rich must live more simply that the poor may simply live."[31] Realistically, we cannot entertain even the illusion that individuals or nations are prepared voluntarily to reduce their intake that the deprived may have enough to survive.

Marxism offers a radical program as the answer to the misery which affects most of the world. It rejects capitalism on both ethical and pragmatic grounds. The core of the Marxist ethical claim is that capitalism is essentially based on egoism and individualistic self-seeking—it maximizes economic gain, raising man's grasping impulse to the point of idealizing the strong and subordinating man to economic production. It presents itself as a democratic system which, say the Marxists, is a cover for unrestricted expansion of individualistic egoism. Capitalism is based on the freedom to acquire property to trade for profit without interference. It makes a virtue of self-seeking, which it acclaims as the most efficient way to produce more for everybody. Self-interest thus becomes the servant of society. The driving force which powers its success derives from competition and laissez-faire in a free market which is self-regulating. Private profit and public welfare become reconciled through impersonal forces of market competition, which leaves individuals to themselves and trusts that their unregulated interactions will produce socially desirable results. Marx himself acknowledged that capitalism led from scarcity to abundance: ". . . in scarce 100 years [capitalism] has created a more massive and more colossal productive force than have all the preceding generations."[32]

This spectacular success in producing abundance is vitiated, say the Marxists, by capitalism's violation of the ethos of human solidarity. It separates people into classes, permitting one of them to feed on the labor of the other; it piously accepts the luxurious life-style of the few who are rich alongside the miserable conditions of the mass of those who are poor. Charles Dickens has left us in his novels a picturesque description of capitalism as it functioned in nineteenth-century England when men cared only for themselves and for what was theirs without any concern about what was happening to others. Capitalism fostered fierce separation among people which is justified by the virtue of bourgeois egoism. Marxism seeks to replace capitalism with a society motivated by the welfare of the total community, a society in which a man will contribute according to his ability, and receive according to his need. It removes the centrality of the individual and replaces him with the ideal of a unified community in which all people are integrally related. It calls for an immediate emancipation of the exploited class and the creation of the new society it envisions.

The prophetic faith and Marxism share several elements in common. Both reject the idea that knowledge is confined to abstract contemplation and insist that its importance lies in concrete engagement as men participate in active relationships to reality. Every member of the good society shares in the possibilities afforded by nature and by human relationships. Both are uncompromising in their opposition to an oppressive and inhuman organization of society; and both require justice as an immediate concrete demand of human existence. They also recognize the need for a historical mediation of the humanist intention, a concrete political and social program supported by an ideological view which moves men to carry forward the work of human liberation. Both the prophets and the Marxists are radical in their confrontation with the existent social order, calling for its restructuring so that the ruling class will be shorn of its oppressive power, and the exploited class will be liberated.

Marxism as interpreted by Lenin, Stalin, Mao, and others can be observed today in Communist countries. It can be discussed in theory and practice. The radicalism of the prophets, however, is obscured by a sacerdotal piety which sanctifies everything in the Bible. Jeremiah's condemnation of the injustices perpetrated in his day was resented by the rulers and powerful landowners. If we would read his radical message today free of its sacrosanct aura, it would draw the fire and denunciation of the conservative owning class. Let us imagine a modern audience listening to this:

Ha! he who builds his house with unfairness and his upper chambers with injustice, who makes his fellowman work without pay and does not give him his wages, who thinks: I will build me a vast palace with spacious upper chambers, provided with windows, paneled in cedar, painted in vermilion! Do you think you are more a king because you compete in cedar? Your father ate and drank, and dispensed justice and equity—then all went well with him. He upheld the rights of the poor and needy—then all was well. That is truly heeding Me. [33]

This was a strong attack upon a way of life which was acceptable to the powerful and silently endured by the weak. It was a way of life in which the rich drenched themselves in ostentatious luxury at the expense of those who worked for them, and whom they robbed of their minimum wages. Anyone who spoke such words today from a soapbox would be called a communist. This same prophet later castigated the rich who in a display of patriotism freed their slaves so that they could go to war against the Babylonian invaders, but re-enslaved them when the battle was over. "Assuredly, thus said the Lord: You would not obey Me and proclaim a release, each to his kinsman and countryman. Lo, I proclaim your release—declares the Lord—to the sword, to pestilence, and to famine: and I will make you a horror to all the kingdoms of the earth." [34] Imagine a modern Jeremiah speaking in Union Square as we sent young men to fight in the Vietnam War and then had no jobs for those who were lucky enough to come home. He would be denounced and called a communist.

The proclamation of the Jubilee Year translated the prophetic call for liberation into divine law. Isaiah had warned: "Ah, those who add house to house, and join field to field, till there is room for none but you to dwell in the land." [35] This radical protest against gobbling up of the land by the rich was enacted in a divine command:

And you shall hallow the fiftieth year. You shall proclaim release throughout the land for all its inhabitants. It shall be a jubilee for you: each of you shall return to his holding, and each of you shall return to his family. . . . But the land must not be sold beyond reclaim, for the land is Mine; you are but strangers with Me. Throughout the land that you hold, you must provide for the redemption of the land. [36]

This provides for the redistribution of land, which in ancient days was the prime measure of wealth, and for the liberation of all serfs and slaves. Men must know that the land belongs to God, who created it, and that all men are his creation and are not servants of other men.

It was not until the last quarter of the nineteenth century that this radical biblical proclamation of the release of the land was formulated into a program for modern society by Henry George. His volume *Progress and Poverty* and his political platform of the Single Tax became the subject of intense discussion as well as political action. Condensed to its basic thesis, George proclaimed equal rights of all men to the land. The land of every country belongs of right to all the people of that country. This right cannot be alienated by one generation so as to affect the title of the next, any more than men can sell their yet-unborn children for slaves. Private ownership of land has no more foundation in morality or reason than private ownership of air or sunlight. This is a secular version of "The land is Mine, said the Lord."

The prophetic faith had resisted institutionalization in biblical days as it does today. There is no room for it in either the Synagogue or the Church. There is no account in the Bible that the Jubilee Year was ever observed—it probably remained then, as it is today, an ideal. It is too radical in its demands upon society to be accommodated, or even tolerated, within the precincts of organized religion. Kings and priests lived comfortably without concern for or protest against the oppression of the widow, the orphan, the stranger, the poor, and the weak in the land. History records the dark, bloody, and horrible acts which have been committed in the name of God. Slavery was justified in ancient days and in the modern age; serfdom was acceptable in the Middle Ages, and in the nineteenth century children were forced to work twelve hours a day for six straight days at starvation wages—all of this and more of the same was sanctioned by the Church and the Synagogue in the name of God. Martin Buber wrote a biting protest against the misuse of the name of God: "What word of human speech," he asks, "is so misused, so defiled, so desecrated as this! All the innocent blood that has been shed for it has robbed it of its radiance. All the injustice it has been used to cover has effaced its features. When I hear the highest called 'God' it sometimes seems blasphemous. . . . It is the most heavy laden of all human words. None has become so soiled, so mistreated. Just for this reason I may not abandon it."[37]

Religion has been co-opted by the present social structure. Marx's well-known statement that religion is the opium of the people may be viewed not so much as an attack upon religion as an appreciation of the comfort it brings to men and women in their misery and suffering as the oppressed class. The promise of pie in the sky, of salvation in a world beyond, enables them to endure injustices and dismiss the idea of rebellion. Charity has become a supremely divine virtue legitimizing the power of the ruling class and leaving the oppressed with a pious wish that their masters will be charitable. The prophetic concept of *tsedakah*, "justice," has been transformed into the religious virtue of charity, which permits the rich to get richer and the poor to get poorer.

As technology became a substitute for human labor, it created a condition which called for social reforms if the capitalist system is to survive. Hours of labor were reduced, children were protected against exploitation, unions were organized to support the laborers' demands for minimum wages and decent working conditions. Religion, however, was not in the forefront of this movement toward relieving the evils of a system which perpetuated exploitation and poverty. In time religious bodies adopted the Social Gospel as an integral part of their faith, and declared themselves on the side of social reform. It is to be noted, however, that the religious community was not unanimous in its acceptance of responsibility for eradicating injustice and exploitation. There were many who insisted that religion must be confined to personal salvation and to the performance of rites and observances hallowed by tradition. At best religious bodies followed the leadership of secular protesters, satisfying their social conscience with resolutions which supported programs initiated by those who suffered exploitation and injustice.

The crux of the matter lies in the shameful fact that religion did not challenge the validity of a society which passively accepted the doctrine that selfish egoism is a virtue. In the present very critical hour of history, religion lives without protest in a social order which separates people into a body of the few endowed with wealth and power, and a mass who are frozen into poverty or at the brink of it.

And what is even more shameful is the blessing which religion bestows upon the profit motive and competition as a noble incentive. It sanctions free enterprise, which in practice allows the powerful to disinherit the weak. An Argentinian peasant-poet satirically describes it.

> They say that God cares for the poor,
> Well, this may be true or not,
> But I know for a fact
> That he dines with the mine owner.

Prophetic faith must be distinguished from *religiosity*, it does not fit into an institution. It declares just one message—God as Creator, and as Liberator of all that is oppressive and enslaving. In an earlier chapter it was noted that both Judaism and Christianity decreed against the appearance of a new prophet since he would represent a threat to the established religious institutions. In our own time Martin Luther King, Jr., who never claimed to be a prophet or the son of a prophet, but whose message was in the Biblical prophetic mold, was, not surprisingly, assassinated.

Secular humanism shares with the Hebrew prophets a commitment to the liberation of men from slavery, oppression, and exploitation. It differs from them in its assertion that man owes his existence to himself, not only materially but emotionally and intellectually as well. Its most profound and elaborate expression was presented by Marx and Engels. It is noteworthy that Marx selected Prometheus as the most important myth in history because it represents rebellion against the gods for the good of mankind. It is the symbol of martyrdom, which is the condition of the proletariat today, and it discloses an unbroken spirit which persists against all threats of disaster. Prometheus is the heroic figure whose purpose and will are to change radically those conditions in which men are oppressed, enslaved, destitute, and despised. The Hebrew prophets would share with Marx his enthusiasm for the Greek myth and its message of human liberation. We have noted above that they hold in common important human values, and perhaps not the least of these is the conviction that solidarity is better than egoism. Both, then, must reject capitalistic egoism and individualistic self-seeking. They affirm together that man's worth is not the single individual, but his integration in a communal unity, and that he can be understood only in relational terms. Both are also exponents of materialism as against idealism in that they deal with the matter of history, the concrete and not the ideal, with the particular historical situation which oppresses the widow, the orphan, the stranger, all the oppressed and the exploited. The prophetic faith has much in common with Marxism, even its rejection of capitalism.

The difference between them is critical and important. Marxism is an elaborate expression of secular humanism which places the responsibility for human liberation in the hands of man, and man alone. The prophetic faith, however, is rooted in ethical monotheism, which binds together human liberation with divine creation. Marxism offers a comprehensive, thoroughgoing secular and autonomous understanding of human existence. It is a missionary ideology which in praxis may be imposed by political power, as exemplified in Russia, China, and other countries today. Its profession of atheism is limited by what Bertrand Russell said of Marx himself: ". . . but he retained the cosmic optimism that only theism can justify."[38] It translates the hopes which men once expressed in religious terms into secular language, and into social programs whose aim is the liberation of man from his enslavement to the past and its burdens. It projects a future of hope for man as a creature of society, and opposes the pessimism which is the mark of existentialists like Nietzsche and Sartre. It declares its faith in mankind, and in this sense may be described as a religion for its affirmation of the value of human existence. Man's destiny is entirely in his own hands, and as is characteristic of classical humanism, he is a creature of creative freedom and of equal worth with all other human beings. It is understandable that in a world disillusioned with its economic, political, and social structure, as well as the general feeling of malaise about the human condition, Marxism as a secular religion is becoming increasingly attractive to many people in the world today.

The present experience of Marxism in praxis reveals the basic fallacy of its claim to the role of liberator of humanity. By its very nature it leads to dictatorship and a denial of personal freedom, excludes popular participation, and lacks the ability to overcome discrimination. By raising man to the status of supreme value as it enshrines humanity instead of God, it has itself become an idolatry—mankind worshipping itself. The biblical prophets were not concerned with atheism, since it was, from all accounts, nonexistent. Their primary target was the evil of idolatry, the worship of gods who were not gods. Deutero-Isaiah poignantly described man chopping down a tree, and after using it for fuel, and for baking bread and roasting meat, "Of the rest he makes a god—his own carving! He bows down to it, worships it; he prays to it and cries, 'Save me, for you are my god.' "[39] Confidence in liberation by man alone "expects both too much and too little," writes Norman Young, "too much of man who constantly turns his creative capacities to destructive ends; too little of God who comes from beyond man's own sphere of management to offer new directions and possibilities."[40]

Marx rejected both idealism and ideology. He scorned idealism because it insists upon mind and spiritual values as fundamental to the world as a whole. It is the opposite of naturalism, which reduces mind and spirit to material things. Kant had made transcendental idealism the popular philosophy of the modern world. He had raised it to an absolute. Marx rejected it entirely, because it failed to recognize that man was being dehumanized and estranged in a bourgeois society; he had become a thing, an object, a mere tool. Idealism can easily become an ideology, which is what happened, said Marx, when capitalism, supported by religion, used it as a weapon against the liberation of the working class. "The basis of the notion of *ideology*," writes Tillich, "is that all psychical and social structures produce an expression in thought which does not possess objective validity, but has only the power of subjective conviction. Thus the idea of transcendence is interpreted as the utopian expression of unsatisfied psychological tendencies, or of unsatisfying social situations. The idea of the absolute becomes the expression of an ultimate need for security."[41] Thus the exploitation of the working people was made acceptable by the promise that in a world beyond, the wrongs committed in this world will be made right. Religion had become an ideology proclaiming a false god, to which the prophets had given the name idolatry, the worship of a self-made god.

Marxism itself fostered communism as an ideology which promised the realization of the utopian society as soon as the proletariat eradicated the bourgeoisie. It projected a secularized version of the Kingdom of God to be brought into being by a radical change in the economic and social structure. It committed the heresy for which the prophets condemned religion—absolutizing the relative. As ideologies both religion and Communism professed utopias as realities, one in a world beyond, the other instantaneously. Both are unrealistic and dangerous. The first is totally outside human experience and beyond either verification or falsification. It is dangerous because it negates all effort on man's part to liberate himself from oppression and to improve his condition on earth. The Communist utopia rests upon the illusion that man will suddenly become a perfected human being. Its most serious neglect is of a realistic understanding of the nature of man. A revolutionary change in the economic and social structure does not usher in the ideal community. Egoism, rivalry, and ethical imbalance are not eradicated so simply! They remain no matter how radically the order is changed. Economic advantage replaces truth, might becomes right, expediency becomes principle, and the interests of a class are identified with those of mankind. Thus ideals came to be worshipped as gods. This is being demonstrated today in those countries which have moved suddenly into a socialized society. Absolute ideology ends in Stalinism, which uses absolute power to compel the good community. By its very nature it must deny personal freedom and suppress all dissent. Religion and Communism share in the heresy of ideology becoming idolatry.

The Biblical prophets were radical realists whose view of the future was conditioned by their understanding of human nature, which inclines man more strongly to do evil than to do good. They themselves accepted the call to prophecy fully aware that despite their fervent plea that men do good and not evil if they would live, the people would not understand it, nor hearken to its divine judgment of doom upon God's chosen people. Their messianic vision of justice and peace reached beyond the immediate context to the end of days, which can be known only by faith. Modern secular prophets separate men into oppressors and liberators; one is the bearer of evil, the other of good. The basic error in this neat scheme is its failure to recognize that the chosen redeeming class becomes, as Niebuhr tells us, "blind to the moral ambiguities of its own acts—demonic self-righteousness—intensified by a utopian illusion. This justifies the use of power over evil doers."[42] Perceptive as Niebuhr's view is, it can be misused to serve a sophisticated rationalization of the status quo, and lead men to work within the established order to mitigate its worst features.

The critically dangerous element in Communism which distinguishes it from the prophetic faith is its failure to recognize the corrupt element in human existence, which is bound to appear on every level of history so long as human freedom is real freedom, and therefore contains the possibility of evil. The failure generates its fanatic fury and prompts its uncritical devotion to the illusion of the immediate realization of the kingdom of righteousness—the classless society.

The disintegration of the bourgeois culture which the Western world is now experiencing, along with the decline of religion, which has become its captive, has moved Marxism to the forefront as an attractive alternative. In one form or another it has been accepted by the most frustrated third of the world's population. Its present failure should not blind us to the possibility that its program for the socialization of property may be a valid, if only a partial, answer to the failure of justice in a highly technological age. The concentration of economic power in the hands of a very few, and the displacement of man by a cybernated scientific machine, lends support to the claim that socialism may be a more effective and humane way of meeting modern man's material needs than the self-interest egoism of capitalism. The present worldwide frustration in the face of the potential of an unlimited abundance testifies to the fact that neither liberal social reformers nor religious declarations of resolutions on social justice are relevant to the radical needs of the modern world. Marxism, where it is practiced, fails when it proclaims its program as the final redemption of history. Father Guilio Girardi, an Italian priest, is appreciated both by churchmen and Communists. "To-day," he writes, "man must see beyond any ingenuous messianism, and become aware of the ambiguous character of the civilization he is building. It holds a great promise and a terrible threat. The promise will be fulfilled and the threat removed only if personal values and subjectivity are given a new lease on life. Consequently, one can understand why socio-economic *praxis* is an excessively partial criterion for judging the validity of a system."[43]

Marxism demonstrates its demonic character in those lands in which it is actualized as an instant Communist utopia. Contemporary Communism is no more Marxist than Western capitalism is Christian. It engages in ruthless persecution, and in an arbitrary denial of human rights, because it fails to take into account the ambiguities of its own self-righteous ideology. In its role as a revolutionary secularistic humanism, it blindly accepts the utopian illusion that man has suddenly achieved perfection. In its drive to overcome the alienation inherent in bourgeois culture, it ignores the fact that it is itself no more than the visualization of alienated people, and is infected with the very alienation it seeks to overcome. Furthermore, the atheistic humanism which is the metaphysical frame in which it defines itself is more absurd than the absurd world in which it proposes to build its utopia. Marxism endows man with those powers which the ancients reserved for their gods, the power to propose and dispose, to create and to liberate, and to act omnipotently and omnisciently. And beyond these illusions it disregards entirely man's supreme alienation—death and transiency. It is becoming clear that changing the social structure by itself fails to answer the dilemma of modern man.

As the twentieth century moves through its final quarter there is an undefined feeling in the air that something immense is dying and something immense is being born. An awareness that a radical change is in the making is not new to history. The Middle Ages, for example, in their waning years, exhibited decadence in the growing intensity of general darkness of mind and spirit, as well as in the misery and suffering of the people. At the same time, however, there were present the beginnings of what ultimately became the brightness of the Renaissance. Such transient periods of history deserve to be called crises. In medical terms a patient is in crisis when the disease which afflicts him can turn either toward better or toward worse. Webster defines "crisis" as an "unstable or crucial time or state of affairs whose outcome will make a decisive difference for better or worse." A careless use of words confounds any problem, and much of what is described today as crisis is hardly a matter of life or death. To speak of an energy crisis at this time is an abuse of the word. There may be less fuel to power our automobiles or to light up Broadway, but these do not constitute a crisis. We may have to face a change in our style of life or endure some inconvenience, but we shall manage to live, less comfortably to be sure. Inflation and unemployment are grim specters, but we shall muddle through more or less painfully. A nuclear holocaust is, probably, the most frightening prospect of all and may be denominated a crisis. But even in this case, the cost is so terribly high for everyone that it acts as a deterrent to an explosion, and thus far it is an uneasy but manageable situation.

The irony in the present hour of social upheaval and economic uncertainty lies in the fact that man is nearer to the realization of his oldest dream than ever before in history. He is practically free of all back-breaking labor, a burden he has assigned to highly sophisticated machines. He also holds in his hands the power to eliminate hunger everywhere in the world, and the ability to satisfy the basic needs of its people. This moment in history is unprecedented—the imminence of enough for everyone. It looks more like the beginning of man than his end. Dickens's lines are more appropriate today than they were when he wrote them in the nineteenth century: "It was the best of times, it was the worst of times; it was the age of wisdom, it was the age of foolishness; it was the spring of hope, it was the winter of despair; we had everything before us, we had nothing before us; we were going direct to heaven, we were going direct the other way."[44]

Two major revolutions are going on in the world today; neither of them was planned, nor did they arrive suddenly—together they constitute the real crisis of the modern world. One of these is the rapid pace of scientific technological advance, which threatens to displace man in the production of goods and services. Eight thousand years separate the agricultural age from the automated technology of today. When the soil was the major source of necessary goods, man harnessed his skill to human and animal power. This provided a minimum standard of living for the majority of people, and a life of plenty and leisure for a very small elite. The industrial age which followed, and which we are now leaving behind, employed human skills to direct machine power. This provided great wealth for a few, a reasonable standard of living for many, and abject poverty for large numbers of people who are unable to find a place in the productive system. We are now at the beginning of the third stage—the cybernetic—in which the production of goods depends upon automated control systems. The machine skill in this stage communicates directions to machine power, replacing much of the human nervous system with automated controls. It is only a hundred years since the machine displaced the human muscle, and now the human nervous system is being disengaged.

The consequent effects of cybernated technology are both impressive and frightening. The possibility of providing adequately for the basic needs of all the people in the world is within reach of this generation. This bright prospect, however, is canceled by man's failure to devise an effective program for the distribution of this rapidly increasing abundance. This failure becomes more dangerous as the rate of population growth moves toward the staggering figure of forty billion, despite all efforts to achieve zero population growth. The earth cannot support that many people, which makes a Malthusian struggle for existence inevitable, a struggle which will be fought with nuclear weapons. The smallest nation will possess atomic-bomb capability as well as the largest, a fact verified today by the proliferation of the ultimate weapon already in progress. The calendar for a nuclear war over limited resources reads something like this: In 1970 it is the politics of despair, in 1980, the politics of desperation, in 1990, the politics of catastrophe, and in the twenty-first century, an era of annihilation.[45]

In addition to this grim prospect is the fact that it now requires fewer people to produce more goods. "Industrial automation has reached the point of no return," writes Richard Bellman of the Rand Corporation; "the pace will increase astronomically in the next decade. Two percent of the population, upper administrative level, will in the discernable future produce all the goods and services needed to feed, clothe, and run our society with the aid of machines."[46] Cybernetic technology is the most iconoclastic of man's inventions, the only one that threatens to replace him. Kurt Vonnegut tells the story of a man who patriotically responds to the call of his country for volunteers to die in order to prevent overpopulation. Before he is put to death he asks whether he will see God, and being assured that he surely will, he excitedly says, "That's good—I've always wanted to ask him a question—what are people for?"[47] The failure to distribute the abundance created by a scientifically sophisticated technology, along with the increasing number of those who are assigned to the heap of useless people, threatens to shatter the basic foundations of our present social order.

Moreover, the sciences—physical, biological, social—are steadily reporting data which add up to "Future Shock." The present rate of exhaustion of natural resources is rapidly reaching the limit of safety. There is a limit to the use of natural resources in support of increased industrial activity. The time varies, but it is not distant when we will be forced to limit our industrial growth in order to survive. Professor Charles Birch, head of the School of Biological Science at the University of Sydney, Australia, summarizes the situation:

> For millions of years the thin envelope of life around the earth, which we call the biosphere, has sustained the resources necessary for its life in a most wonderful and complex way. Every molecule of oxygen in the atmosphere comes from the plants. Every time you take a breath you can say thank you to a plant. All the oxygen is completely recycled by living organisms every 2000 years. Every molecule of carbon-dioxide in the air, soil, and water comes from living organisms. All the carbon-dioxide is renewed every 300 years. Every molecule of water on this planet goes in and out of living organisms. All the water is renewed completely every 22 million years. Nature's global society is a sustainable society. It keeps the molecules moving. We had better keep it that way if we want to stay around.[48]

It is not the biosphere alone which is fatally threatened. The ecosphere, the environment itself, cannot absorb the increased heat which is poured into the atmosphere by our increasing use of energy. Even if we succeed in obtaining new sources of energy from the sun, wind, or water, its use emits heat. The more industrial growth that takes place, the more polluted the environment becomes, to the point ultimately where life can no longer exist within it.

> In the developed world industrial production has been growing at a rate of about 7 percent a year, thereby doubling every ten years. If we project this growth rate for another fifty years, it would follow that the demand for resources would have doubled five times, requiring a volume of resource extraction thirty times larger than today's; and if we look ahead over the ten doublings of a century, the amount of annual resource requirements would have increased by over a thousand times. [49]

The thermal pollution in our industrial age presents us with the most lethal threat to human existence on our planet.

The scientist's role as a prophet of doom is a surprising turnabout since his voice in the past had announced the near-approach of utopia. The popular response to his grim prophecy is not unlike that which greeted the Hebrew prophets when they predicted the catastrophic fall of both Israel and Judah. The people placed their confidence in *Yom Yahweh*, the Day of the Lord. For them it was the day of redemption, a day when their God would defeat their enemies and bring victory, peace, and prosperity. They learned with disastrous reality, however, that the Day of the Lord is the day of judgment and not salvation. Both Israel and Judah fell. It was not, however, the end of the people of Israel, much less of all humanity.

The confident response to the scientist's prophecy of doom today rests upon modern man's faith in science itself. The threatening problems which science has created, science can resolve. Clarence Ayres, professor of economics at the University of Texas, warned us that science is a false Messiah. [50] The brilliant promise of scientifically sophisticated technology, so rich in its potential for great good, is moving all humanity, all of life, to its irrecoverable end on earth. The first major revolution of our time, then, the rapid development of science, is leading toward the crisis which can turn into the final holocaust.

The other revolution, taking place concurrently with the first, is the unplanned steady shift from theism to secularism. The implications of a radical change from one *weltanschauung* to another are critically serious, and when, as today, the change is linked to the new scientific revolution, it adds up to the supreme, and possibly the final, crisis of humankind. Theistic faith, now giving way to secularism, postulates the view that the universe is the outflow of one ultimate reality, that one universal will permeates nature, history, and morality. In this view man is a rational creature, endowed with freedom, and potentially creative. These characteristics of his nature are a reflection of the Being of all beings. The world in which man lives is orderly and is both rational and intelligible. Essentially, this constitutes the heart of the God-faith, which is expressed in a variety of forms, and bears the stamp of different theological formulations. The previous chapter discusses the difference between classical and neoclassical theism. The implications of the theistic view of the universe are common to all its different forms. It holds the belief that man is a significant being whose existence is endowed with purpose, and that he is a creature of cosmic worth in his individual being as well as in his natural kinship with all other men. His life is goal-directed, and his fulfillment is achieved as he becomes fully rational, creative, free, and good. These characteristics of man, in the theistic view, are not a matter of caprice lost in subjectivity, they are an inseparable part of being itself.

Secularism, which is increasingly dominating modern culture, posits a universe which is an accidental concantenation of atoms devoid of purpose or goal. Athough its natural laws operate efficiently and dependably, they are part of an absurd nothingness, "a tale told by an idiot." Milton Steinberg compared it to a "madman who breathes, injests, and secretes regularly, whose body conforms to the normal, rational pattern of all living things. Yet he is insane in that his actions are without intelligible objective and recognizable purpose."[51] Secularists, not unlike theists, differ among themselves in their interpretation of their basic view of the universe. The implications of their secularistic *weltanschauung* are as clear as those of theism. In this view man is a things among things, a by-product of a blind machine. He is endowed with capacities to love, to think, to show compassion; he is nevertheless a freak of the universe, or as Bertrand Russell describes him, "the phosphorescence of slime." He is without dignity or worth, and his significance is no more than that of a cockroach. Sartre, who found the world absurd, logically concluded that man's birth is absurd, and his death is absurd. His relationship to other human beings is not one of kinship, but of fierce separation, since there is no one being in whom they all participate. Experience may temper strife and violence, but it cannot create a harmonious human community. Human existence, in the secularist view, is a journey from nowhere to nowhere in which man is free to make the best of it. "The individual," says Steinberg, "an infinitesimal syllable in this idiot's tale must take such comfort as he can from the chance experience allowed him in the pointless interval of consciousness between the mysterious dawn and an equally mysterious dusk."[52]

T. S. Eliot announced the change from theism to secularism in these lines: "But it seems something is happening that never happened before . . . Men have left God, not for other gods, they say, but for no God, and this has never happened before."[53] The critical issue today is radically different from anything man has experienced in the past—is a secularist view of the universe adequate to meet the responsibilities created for him by the new scientific revolution Human survival now depends upon an ethics in a new key, an ethics which must reach beyond the traditional ideal that man should love his neighbor as himself. At this point in history man has not yet decided who his neighbor is. Some exclude people with different-colored skins, or people of another economic or social class, or those of another national or religious community. The fact is that modern man, far from living by the morality of love of neighbor, lives today with an uneasy hope that the universal fear of total destruction will lead all men to an ethics of expediency. Fear of neighbor has become the morality of survival. The possibility is always present that someone may choose to gamble and take the risk of blowing his neighbor to pieces in order to capture a little of the constantly depleting stock of natural resources. An ethics based on fear and expediency is woefully inadequate in the present human condition.

The present generation is acting prudently, and managing to survive with greater or lesser dislocation. Its children, grandchildren, and even great-grandchildren may be spared the final holocaust by a morality of expediency motivated by fear. If, however, man persists in his present life-style, he must sooner or later reach the limit beyond which life on earth is no longer possible. This may come a century hence, or two or even ten. "Supposing we knew with a high degree of certainty," asks Robert Heilbroner, "that humankind could not survive a thousand years unless we gave up our wasteful diet of meat, abandon all pleasure driving, cut back on every use of energy that was not essential to a bare minimum, would we care enough for posterity to pay the price for its survival? I doubt it."[54] It is an impossible question and an outrageous answer. Most people could not live with the *conscious* knowledge that their continuing consumption of goods beyond the minimum necessary for existence is contributing to the end of all life on earth, whether in a hundred years or a thousand. No one is ready to curse unborn generations with an easy, "To hell with you." Yet that is exactly what most of us are doing! The present crisis calls for an ethics beyond expediency through fear, and even higher than love of neighbor now living on earth. Confronted with a real threat to the existence of all life on earth, man desperately needs an ethics which compels him to accept the responsibility for the enormous sacrifices which human survival beyond the present hour of history demands. Our dilemma today is that we do know, or we can know, what must be done in order to avoid the end of the world. Human intelligence can devise a program of restraint against the exploitation of nature and of men. What we lack, as Toulmin tells us, is the ability to put our hearts into it; i.e., the religious dimension of life.

Modern man is living in an axial period of history, a time when an old culture is dying and a new culture is straining painfully to be born. For the first time in history an end to all of life on earth looms ahead in a not-too-distant future. Two major revolutions, described above, are largely responsible for the movement toward a final holocaust, and both continue with increased intensity and subtle deceptivity. Scientific technology is confidently heralded as the unending source of new inventions which will meet all of man's most critical needs now and forever. The subtle deception of this faith in science lies in its very brilliant success story, since it is itself the primary cause for the final disaster—and, in a similar way, the radical change from theism to secularism comes disguised by a culture which venerates religion enculturated by the Secular City, which has co-opted God and put him on call. "It is a question," writes Hans Jonas, "whether without restoring the category of the sacred, the category most thoroughly destroyed by the scientific enlightenment, we can have an ethics able to cope with the extreme powers which we possess today and constantly increase and are almost compelled to use."[55]

The supreme need in this hour of crisis is an ethics which will move men to accept responsibility for the survival of human existence in an unborn future. Secular humanism, in both its melioristic and revolutionary forms, has proved itself pitifully inadequate of overcoming the gigantic threat to the continuation of life on earth. That there has been a small measure of social progress which has liberated man from some oppression is undeniable. Commonsense wisdom should encourage increased efforts in the work of improving the conditions of human existence. We should not lose sight, however, of the grim fact that despite our noble, though modest efforts, most of the people of the world are hungry amid plenty, oppressed despite declarations of human rights, and exploited by giant corporate power which is impersonal and often invisible. Nevertheless, men and women of good will should join together in the practical work of liberation wherever people are enslaved by poverty, tyranny, or the ruthless use of power. The ethics which motivates this work of social progress varies from simple expediency to the ideal of love of neighbor. Praiseworthy as this work is, and important in relieving suffering, it is wholly inadequate to move men to confront the realistic threat of human extinction which is already a foreseeable future.

The prophetic faith in the neoclassical frame, described in the previous chapter, offers modern man an ethics acceptable to the present cultural milieu, and morally responsible in the life-and-death crisis he must resolve. Its program is more radical than social meliorism, and more profound than the secular revolutionary program advanced by Marxists. The prophetic faith is different in its recognition of the important, inescapable fact that liberation without creation is both inadequate and dangerous. When man assumes the role of the sole creator of history, and himself becomes the supreme value, he is practicing idolatry. Being human he is frustrated and discouraged when his best efforts fail. He soon rejects his role as creator and, as Erich Fromm reminded us, seeks an escape from freedom. The natural consequence, as history has recently demonstrated, is that he submits to the dictatorial authority of a Stalin or a Hitler.

The fatal defect in secular humanism is its rejection of the transcendent. In today's postmodern culture this term does not describe a spatial dimension, something *out there*. There is, as has been noted above, the transcendent One, which is at the same time immanent with an infinite qualitative difference. Finitude is part of infinity. Without the transcendent that loves, prehends, persuades, and preserves, the most ideal humanism deceives itself. Tillich prefers the term "supra-temporal," which is not as satisfactory as "transcendent-immanent" because it suggests a greater distinction than is real. He makes an important point, however, which is central to this discussion.

> Social justice is incomplete and mechanistic where love does not give life and creative power. Heroism deceives itself if it does not see that in its devotion to the future which it does not experience it contains a supra-temporal element, and it is precisely this element which gives to heroism its dignity and its power of giving meaning to life. . . . without such a supra-temporal element social heroism is condemned to swinging back and forth between utopianism and resignation.[56]

Secular humanism without any relation to a transcendent reality is not only inadequate to meet the threat to the survival of future generations, it is helpless, even dangerous, when applied to the immediate needs of the world today. It is unfortunate that this appeal to the transcendent lends itself to serious misunderstanding among theists themselves. In the present hour of political, social, and moral confusion, classical religionists are passionately calling for a return to God, whom they endow with omnipotence, omniscience, and love. They accept him despite his failure to use his omnipotent power to prevent the mass murder of millions of innocent men, women, and children in Auschwitz. Such a God is for other theists a monster. Most liberation theologians today, whether in Latin America or the blacks in America, have not resolved the painful inconsistency in their understanding of God. What is being suggested here is the proposition that the prophetic faith, freed of its classical theological formulation, confronts us with a God who is creator as he liberates, and is transcendent as he is immanent.

The message which modern man needs to hear above all others is that he is not alone, that the meaning of his existence lies in his relationship to the *whole* in which there is the supreme creativity, God. This also implies that there is a goal toward which all creation moves, a goal which God alone cannot achieve. He can propose, but man, being free, can dispose. The primary function of religion is to provide an answer to the meaning of human existence. Science investigates the laws of nature, philosophy seeks answers to questions raised by reason and logic, aesthetics aims at defining beauty. Religion, from the earliest historical forms to the present postmodern formulation, gives an answer to the question which man innately asks—what is the *meaning* of my existence?

The Hebrew prophets taught the doctrine that the only reason for human existence is to be a co-worker with God the creator to move history toward that end which was planned from the beginning. As the only creature in the long evolution of life on earth who is conscious of his self and what lies beyond it, man can comprehend creation, purpose, and goal. The fulfillment of the divine plan is the only reason for human existence. The prophets did not raise the question of whether God, the omnipotent, can do it alone, without man. They recognized that neither man nor God can do it alone. Their *weltanschauung* endows man with a responsibility that reaches into the unforeseeable future, and demands an ethics adequate for a man's role in the present crisis. The way to begin fulfilling his role man is told: "You must love the Lord your God with all your heart and with all your soul and with all your might. Take to heart these words which I charge you this day."[57] This succinctly defines the prophetic view of man's reason for being—to so love God the creator that we will respond to his proposal and do that which will bring humanity nearer to the Kingdom of God.

But man is such a weak reed upon whom the creator must lean. Historically man's record reveals that he chooses most often to ignore God's proposals. The slow movement from the amoeba to Einstein argues for a millennial patient confidence in the future. But time, it seems, is running out. Doomsday in a scientific age is very real and may be actualized within the lifetime of our grandchildren. The mood of despair which dominates our culture testifies to the hopelessness that darkens man's soul. The hope that God will intervene to save us is alien to modern culture; it was alien even to the Biblical prophets. They did not spare Israel the brutal picture of what lay ahead. "Hear this word which I intoned as a dirge over you, O House of Israel: Fallen, not to rise again, is Maiden Israel; abandoned on her soil, with none to lift her up."[58] This is a prophecy of ultimate and final doom without any hope of redemption.

The prophet of this prophecy of unredeemable doom went on to say: "Thus said the Lord to the House of Israel: Seek me, and you will live . . . Seek the Lord and you will live."[59] A prophetic voice concludes the Book of Amos with a positive assurance for the restoration of Israel: "I will restore my people Israel. They shall rebuild ruined cities and inhabit them; they shall plant vineyards and drink wine; they shall till gardens and eat their fruits. And I will plant them upon the soil. Never more to be uprooted from the soil I have given them—Said the Lord your God."[60] This prophet and all the others who pronounced doom never allowed it to be the last word. Their prophecies were fulfilled, both Israel and Judah were conquered and driven into exile. But it was not the end; God could not be defeated in his plans for Israel's role in the achievement of his kingdom on earth. The prophets do not tell us how it happened, how this people who rejected God's pleadings, threats, and judgments is redeemed and restored to life. The prophetic faith was rooted in the confident assurance that divine victory shall come in the end of days. Modern man's faith cannot be so confident, since the final holocaust promises to be so utterly complete that divine restoration will become impossible, since God himself must suffer the fate of the whole, the One of which he is a part, of all that exists. The eternal is lost in the finite.

Faith in God, however, whose reality, as Ogden has reminded us, lies "in our ineradicable confidence in the final worth of existence," arouses within us a profound trust that the judgment can be realized. The prophetic faith in the neoclassic formulation can awaken within modern man the confidence that in the face of the threat of the end of all life on earth, there is yet time to be persuaded by God and live. Furthermore, God in his consequent nature assures us that nothing is lost, that all is prehended and becomes part of the immediacy of his own life. The knowledge and the feeling that God's tender care is ever-present supports our confidence in the value of life, and thus is a compelling motivation to respond to his loving call, and to be persuaded. The radical change which man is called upon to make is the understanding of the meaning of his own existence. If he is persuaded that he is an integral part of an interrelational *whole* and the ONE whose purpose is creation through liberation, then he can fashion an ethics adequate to meet the life-and-death crisis in which he lives today. Ethical monotheism, understood in the neoclassical formulation described in a previous chapter, is the prophetic faith which can strengthen man's confidence that he is not alone in his struggle to save himself from the impending final holocaust. This will require a covenanted community fiercely passionate in its witness to God who as Creator is Liberator.

Notes

INTRODUCTION

1. Reinhold Niebuhr, *Faith and History* (New York, 1959) p. vii.

2. E. F. Magnin, "The Voice of Prophecy in This Satellite Age," in *Interpreting the Prophetic Tradition* (Cincinnati, 1969) pp. 104–105.

3. Van A. Harvey, *The Historian and the Believer* (New York, 1966), pp. 114–115.

4. Ibid., p. 3.

5. Jeremiah 51:11.

6. Isaiah 44:28.

7. H. H. Rowley, *The Relevance of the Bible* (New York, 1944) pp. 17–18.

CHAPTER 1

1. R. Hazelton, *A Theological Approach to Art* (Nashville, 1967) p. 57.

2. B. Shahn, *The Biography of a Painting: Creativity in the Arts*, p. 28, quoted by Hazelton, p. 121.

3. S. Freud, *Autobiography*, trans. Strachen (New York, 1953), p. 133.

4. Hazelton, op. cit.

5. Ibn Ezra, *M. Shireth Israel* (Berlin, 1921), p. 45, quoted by A. J. Heschel, *The Prophets* (New York, 1969), p. 38.

6. Exodus 15:20–21.

7. Judges 4:4, 5:1.

8. II Samuel 23:1–3.

9. Ezekiel 21:5.

10. Ibid. 33:32.

11. M. Buttenweiser, *The Prophets of Israel* (New York, 1914), p. 156.

12. Plato, *Dialogues*, trans. Jowett, (New York), 1:289 ff.

13. Plato, *Apology*, ibid., p. 405.

14. Hesiod, *Theogony*, 131 ff.

15. Aristotle, *Poeticus* XVII, 2, trans. Fyfe (Oxford, 1940).

16. B. Croce, *Aesthetics* (London, 1929), p. 51.

17. J. W. Goethe, *Conversations and Encounters*, ed. Luke and Pick (Chicago, 1966), p. 177.

18. F. Nietzsche, "Composition of *Thus Spake Zarathustra*," trans. Fadiman, in *Creative Process: A Symposium*, ed. Ghuselin (Los Angeles: University of California Press, 1952), pp. 209 ff.

19. A. Lowell, "Process of Making Poetry," in Ghuselin, op. cit, p. 111.
20. Ibid., p. 110
21. Ibid., p. 111.
22. S. Spender, "The Making of a Poem," in Ghuselin, op. cit., p. 119.
23. G. Keynes, ed., *Letters of William Blake* (London, 1956).
24. E. Jones, *Hamlet and Oedipus* (New York, 1949), pp. 15 ff.
25. E. M. Harding, *An Anatomy of Inspiration* (Cambridge, 1948), p. 17.
26. G. Berger, *Toward Reality* (New York, 1962), p. 57.
27. Hazelton, op. cit., p. 122.
28. Isaiah 6:9.
29. Exodus 2:11 ff.
30. M. R. Rilke, *The Notebooks of Malte Lauride Brigge* (New York, 1949), pp. 26 ff.
31. W. J. H. B. Sandberg, "Picasso's *Guernica*," *Daedalus* (Winter 1960), p. 245.
32. Amos 2:6.
33. A. Rattner, *Twenty-four Plates*, Intr. and Notes by Weller (Urbana: University of Chicago Press, 1945), p. 6.
34. Ibid., p. 4.
35. Ibid., p. 4.
36. Isaiah 55:2.
37. Quoted by Roger L. Shinn, "The Artist as Prophet-Priest of Culture," in *Christian Faith and Contemporary Arts*, ed. F. Eversole (Nashville, 1926), p. 78.
38. Ibid., p. 72.
39. *New York Times*, June 1973, p. 3.
40. Amos 3:8.
41. J. Portnoy, "Is the Creative Process Similar in the Arts," op. cit., note 37.
42. R. Ortmayer, "Art Beyond Celebration," in ibid., p. 195.
43. Ibid., p. 198.
44. T. S. Eliot, in ibid., p. 51.
45. Hosea 11:1–8.
46. Proverbs 3:12.
47. National Council of Churches, *Report on Art*, p. 6.
48. G. Burger, *Toward Reality* (New York, 1962), p. xvi.
49. G. B. Shaw, *Atlantic Monthly* 226, no. 3 (September 1970): 90.
50. Hosea 9:13–14.
51. Hosea 14:2, 6, 10.
52. W. Kandinsky, *Concerning the Spiritual in Art* (New York, 1955), pp. 23 ff.
53. W. B. Yeats, "The Second Coming," in *Collected Poems* (New York, 1952), p. 184.
54. S. Kierkegaard, *The Point of View For My Work as an Author*, trans. W. Lowrie (New York, 1962), pp. 68 ff.
55. B. Spinoza, *Ethics*, prop. XVII, ed. G. Gutmann (New York, 1949), p. 224.
56. S. Kierkegaard, *On Authority and Revelation*, trans. Lowrie (Princeton, 1955), p. 22.
57. Ibid., p. 73.
58. S. Kierkegaard, *Journal* (Oxford University Press, 1938), p. 885.
59. S. Kierkegaard, *The Present Age to Alexander* (London, 1940), pp. 146–147.
60. Isaiah 55:8–9.
61. S. Kierkegaard, *On Authority and Revelation*, p. 22.

62. L. Hobhouse, in my personal notes without reference.
63. F. Dostoevsky, *Notes From the Underground*; quotation from G. Steiner, *Tolstoy and Dostoevsky* (1959), p. 227.
64. Ibid., p. 226.
65. Amos 5:18.
66. Jeremiah 7:13–15.
67. B. Bamberger, personal correspondence.
68. Micah 6:6–8.
69. W. Hubben, *Dostoevsky, Kierkegaard, Nietzsche, and Kafka* (New York, 1969), p. 22.
70. Ibid., p. 84.
71. Ibid., p. 85.
72. Isaiah 10:5–6.
73. Amos 7:12.
74. W. Lowrie, *Kierkegaard* (New York, 1962), 2:22.
75. Isaiah, 1:5–6.
76. D. Bell, "Technology, Nature, and Society," *American Scholar* 42 (Summer 1973): 403.

CHAPTER 2

1. *Ancient Near East Supplementary Texts and Pictures*, ed. J. B. Pritchard (1969), pp. 187–191. Also, "Prophecy in Hamath, Israel and Mari," *Harvard Theological Review* 63, (1970): 1–28.
2. I Samuel 9:9.
3. Ibid. 10:5–12.
4. R. B. Y. Scott, *The Relevance of the Prophecy* (New York, 1952).
5. I Samuel 8:11–18.
6. II Samuel 11:2–12, 15.
7. I Kings 18:17–18.
8. Jeremiah 35:1–11.
9. I Kings 22:5–23.
10. Hosea 2:17.
11. Jeremiah 2.13.
12. Hosea 4:6.
13. J. Skinner, *Prophecy and Religion* (London, 1936), pp. 195–196.
14. Deuteronomy 34:10.
15. Isaiah 6:1–8.
16. Jeremiah 1:5.
17. G. W. Povah, *The New Psychology and the Hebrew Prophets* (London, 1925), p. 114.
18. W. Shakespeare, *Hamlet*, act I scene 5.
19. Jeremiah 1:6.
20. Jeremiah 15:17.
21. W. Shakespeare, *Hamlet,* act III scene 1.
22. Jeremiah 15:10.
23. Jeremiah 20:7–9.
24. W. C. Klein, *The Psychological Pattern of the Old Testament Prophecy* (Evanston, Ill., 1956), p. 31.

25. Ibid., p. 73.
26. Ibid., p. 70.
27. S. Freud, *An Autobiographical Study*, trans. G. Strachey, 2 ed. (1946), pp. 119–120.
28. Isaiah 6:9.
29. Jeremiah 9:10–11.
30. Scott, op. cit., p. 13.
31. W. F. Albright, *Samuel and the Beginnings of the Prophetic Movement in Interpretating the Prophetic Tradition* (Cincinnati, 1969), p. 151.
32. Ezekiel 2:4–5.
33. Ezekiel 3:16–21.
34. Amos 3:7.
35. R. B. Y. Scott, *The Way of Wisdom* (New York, 1971), pp. 113 ff.
36. H. C. Ackerman, "The Nature of Hebrew Prophecy," *Anglican Theological Review* 4 (1921–22): 103.
37. Amos 7:2–3.
38. Isaiah 22:4.
39. Jeremiah 14:7–9, 15:1–2.
40. Genesis 27:1–46.
41. Judges 11:29–40.
42. Psalms 147:15.
43. Jeremiah 23:29.
44. Zechariah 1:6.
45. Isaiah 55:10–11.
46. Genesis 1:3.
47. Psalms 33:6, 9.
48. Wisdom of Solomon 18:15–16 (Revised Standard Version).
49. Jeremiah 1:9–10.
50. G. F. Moore, *Judaism* (Cambridge, 1927), 1:414.
51. Amos 7:10.
52. W. J. Moore, "A Study of the Concept of the Mighty Word in Ancient Hebrew Literature," dissertation (University of Chicago Libraries, 1946), pp. 2 ff.
53. B. Shahn, *Love and Joy about Letters*, (New York, 1963), p. 5.
54. Ibid., pp. 18–19, illustrations, pp. 36–37.
55. Leviticus 10:10.
56. II Samuel 6:6–7.
57. Isaiah 49:2.
58. Amos 8:1–2.
59. Jeremiah 1:11.
60. H. C. Brichto, "On Faith and Revelation in the Bible," *Hebrew Union College Annual* 39 (1968): 52.
61. Jeremiah 28:1–17.
62. II Kings 22:5–23.
63. Isaiah 28:7.
64. Micah 3:11.
65. Micah 3:5.
66. Jeremiah 2:8, 5:31, 23:14.
67. Jeremiah 28:15–16.

68. Ezekiel 13:1–7.
69. Deuteronomy 18:21.
70. Deuteronomy 13:24.
71. Amos, chaps. 1 and 2.
72. M. Buber, *The Prophetic Faith* (New York: Harper Torchbooks, 1949), p. 178.
73. Isaiah 31:5, 33:17–22.
74. J. H. Crenshaw, *Prophetic Conflict* (New York, 1971), p. 17.
75. Jeremiah 28:15.
76. T. W. Overholt, "The Question of False Prophecy," *Journal of the American Academy of Religion* 35 (September 1967): 248.
77. Ibid.
78. A. Boisen, quoted by Seward Hiltner in *Religion in Life* 41 (Autumn 1972): 412 ff.

CHAPTER 3
1. N. H. Glatzer, "A Study of the Interpretation of Prophecy," *Review of Religions* 10 (1946): 115.
2. L. Ginzberg, *The Legends of the Jews* (Philadelphia, 1928), 6:448.
3. I Macc. 4:46.
4. Ibid. 14:41.
5. Ibid. 9:27.
6. G. F. Moore, *Judaism* (Cambridge, Mass., 1927), 1:240.
7. Psalms 74:9.
8. Zechariah 13:3 ff.
9. Josephus, *Ant*. XVIII 4:1, XX 5:1, 8:10.
10. Glatzer, op. cit., p. 116.
11. S. Tedesche and S. Zeitlin, *The First Book of Maccabees* (Dropsie College edition, 1950), p. x.
12. R. H. Charles, *Religious Development Between Old and New Testaments*, p. 195.
13. J. Bloch, *On the Apocalyptic in Judaism* (Jewish Quarterly Review Monograph no. 11, Philadelphia, 1952).
14. *Pirke Aboth* I:1.
15. H. A. Fischel, *The Rabbinic Conception of Prophecy* (Edinburgh, 1944), p. 31.
16. Jer. *Megillah* 70d.
17. Fischel, op. cit., pp. 32–36.
18. *Sukkah* 49b.
19. Jer. Berakot 8d.
20. *Pesikta*, ed. Buber, 140b.
21. *Mekilta* on Exodus 14:31.
22. *Exodus R*. 32:1.
23. *Mekilta* on Exodus 15:2.
24. *Baba Mezia* 59b.
25. *Erubin* 63a.
26. *Exodus R*. 29:9, end.
27. Daniel 4:28.

28. Matt. 3:17.
29. *Cant. R.* 8:11.
30. Glatzer, op. cit., p. 124.
31. Tos. *Sotah* 13:3 ff.
32. Ibid.; also in *Sotah* 48b, *Sanhedrin* 11a.
33. Tos. *Sotah* 13:2.
34. Acts 3:24.
35. Justin, *Dialogue*, Chap. 7; quoted by Glatzer, op. cit., p. 116.
36. *Gen. R.* 41:42.
37. *Pesikta Rab.*, ed. Friedman, 136a.
38. *Megillah* 14a.
39. Glatzer, op. cit., p. 125.
40. *Ecc. R.* 1:34.
41. Zechariah 14:9.
42. *Timaeus* 71E.
43. Genesis 15:12.
44. *Heres* 51:249, 52:258, 53:264.
45. H. A. Wolfson, *Philo* (Cambridge, Mass., 1947), 2:27.
46. Philo, *Gig.* 13:60.
47. Wolfson, op. cit., p. 28.
48. Ibid., p. 31.
49. Exodus 33:11.
50. *Decal.* 9:32–35; also Wolfson, op. cit., pp. 36–38.
51. H. A. Wolfson, "Halevi and Maimonides on Prophecy," *Jewish Quarterly Review* 32 1941–42: 345–370, and 33 (1942–43): 49–82.
52. *Cuzari* I 95.
53. Ibid. 87.
54. *De Decalogo* 9:33.
55. *Cuzari* I 89.
56. Ibid. II 4.
57. Ibid. I 95.
58. Maimonides, *Moreh Nebukin* II 32.
59. Ibid. II 36.
60. *Mishne Torah, Yesode Ha-Torah* VIII 6; Introduction to *Perek Helek*, article 7.
61. *Moreh Nebukim* II 33.
62. *Encyclopedia of Philosophy* (New York, 1967), p. 132.
63. *Iggeret Teman*, Kolheg, II, p. 4a.
64. *Moreh Nebukim* II 45.
65. Numbers 12:6.
66. Genesis 15:12.
67. Exodus 3:11
68. *Mishne Torah, Yesode Ha-Torah* VII 2, 6.
69. Daniel 10:8.
70. *Moreh Nebukim* II 41. See also Abraham J. Heschel, *The Prophets* (New York, 1962), pp. 340 ff.
71. *Moreh Nebukim* I 40, II 45(1), and II 6.
72. C. Brinton, *Ideas and Men* (New York, 1950), p. 256.

73. St. Thomas Aquinas, *Summa Contra Gentiles*, IV, chap. 1.

74. L. Strauss, *Philosophie und Gesetz* (Berlin, 1935), pp. 76 ff.

75. Ibid., p. 122.

76. Quoted by S. H. Bergmann, "God and Man in Modern Thought," *Judaism* 6 (Spring 1957): 99–109.

77. Ibid.

78. *Tractatus Theologicus Politicus* IV, chap. XV.

79. J. Guttmann, *Philosophies of Judaism*, trans. by W. Silverman (London, 1964), pp. 282–285.

80. Spinoza, op. cit., I, 7–44, also II, 17 (German edition, Bruder).

81. J. Locke, *Concerning Human Understanding*, ed. A. S. Pringle-Pattison, (Oxford, 1934), IV, chap. 19.

82. Ibid., p. 356.

83. Ibid., pp. 357–358.

84. Ibid.

85. Ibid., p. 9.

86. Ibid., pp. 360–363.

87. Ibid.

88. J. Locke, *A Discourse of Miracle—Reasonableness of Christianity*, ed. I. T. Ramsey, Stanford edition, p. 80.

89. I. Kant, *What Is Enlightenment?* trans. and ed. L. W. Beck (Chicago, 1955), p. 286.

90. *Kritik der Reinan Verkunft*, Preface to 2d edition; quoted by John Baillie, *The Idea of Revelation in Recent Thought* (New York, 1956), pp. 9–10.

91. Quoted by Bergmann, op. cit.

92. Ibid.

93. Ibid.

94. Ibid.

95. J. G. Fichte, 5th and 6th Lectures, quoted by Bergmann, ibid.

96. Ibid.

97. D. Hume, *Dialogues Concerning Natural Religion*, XII.

98. L. Silberman, "Prophets and Philosophers," in *Interpreting the Prophetic Tradition* (Cincinnati, 1969), p. 81.

99. H. Cohen, in S. Bergmann, *Faith and Reason*, trans. and ed. by Jospe (Washington, D.C., 1961), p. 35.

100. Ibid., p. 36.

101. Ibid., p. 39.

102. B. Jowett, "On the Interpretation of Scripture," in *Essays and Reviews*, 10th ed. (London, 1926).

103. Jeremiah 15:19.

104. S. T. Coleridge, *Confessions of an Inquiring Spirit*, Letter I.

105. *De Principiis* IV 6, trans. Gwatkin, *Selections from Early Christian Writers* LI a.

106. W. Temple, *Revelation*, ed. Baillis and Martin (London, 1937), p. 138.

107. S. S. Cohon, *Jewish Theology* (Assen, Netherlands, 1971), p. 138.

108. Amos 3:7.

109. H. W. Robinson, *Inspiration* (Oxford, 1946), p. 193.

110. Ibid.

111. A. N. Whitehead, *Religion in the Making* (New York, 1957), p. 58.

112. K. Barth, *Church Dogmatics*, ed. Bromley and Torrence (1952), 1:124.

113. E. Brunner, *The Word and the World* (Lexington, Ky., 1905), p. 97.

114. Ibid.

115. R. Bultmann, "How Does God Speak Through the Bible," in *Existence and Faith*, trans. Schubert Ogden (New York, 1960), p. 170.

116. Ibid., p. 168.

117. M. Buber, *On the Bible*, ed. Nahum M. Glatzer, (New York, 1968), p. 4.

118. Reinhold Niebuhr,

119. Isaiah 29:11–12.

CHAPTER 4

1. W. A. Irwin, *The Old Testament: Keystone of Human Culture*, (New York, 1952), pp. 54–55.

2. Isaiah 40:12–14, 26.

3. Isaiah 42:6.

4. B. Malinowski, in *Encyclopedia of Social Science*, 4:621.

5. V. A. Harvey, *A Handbook of Theological Terms* (New York, 1964), p. 235.

6. H. D. Lubac, *The Discovery of God* (New York, 1960), p. 167.

7. S. Toulmin, *An Examination of the Place of Reason in Ethics* (Cambridge University Press, 1950), p. 219.

8. Quoted by Huston Smith in the *Hartshorne Festschrift* (La Salle, 1964), p. 41.

9. M. Heidegger, *Being and Time*, trans. Macquarrie-Robinson (New York, 1962), pp. 163 ff.

10. H. Schilling, *The New Consciousness of Science and Religion* (Philadelphia, 1973), p. 26.

11. A. N. Whitehead, *Modes of Thought* (New York, 1938), p. 146.

12. S. Ogden, *The Reality of God* (New York, 1963), p. 29.

13. A. N. Whitehead, *Religion in the Making* (New York, 1926), p. 119, and *Modes of Thought*, pp. 117 ff.

14. John Dewey, *Human Nature and Conduct* (New York, 1928), p. 331.

15. B. Russell, *Why I Am Not a Christian* (New York, 1957), p. 197.

16. J. Huxley, *Religion Without Revelation* (London, 1957), pp. 58, 62.

17. J. P. Sartre, *Commentary on "Being and Nothingness,"* by J. Catalano (1974), p. 21.

18. J. Huxley, *Essays of a Humanist* (New York, 1964), p. 112.

19. K. Barth, *Church Dogmatics* (Edinburgh, 1957), p. 561.

20. A. D. Gallaway, "A God I Can Talk To," in *God, Secularization and History*, ed. E. T. Lane (University of Southern California, 1974), p. 114.

21. Amos 3:6.

22. Isaiah 45:7.

23. M. Buber, Review of *On Judaism*, *Saturday Review of Literature*, February 10, 1968, p. 34.

24. C. Hartshorne, *Divine Relativity* (New Haven, 1948), p. 80.

25. A. J. Heschel, *The Prophets* (Philadelphia, 1962), p. 260.

26. F. R. Tenant, *Philosophical Theology* (Cambridge, 1930), 2:166.

27. J. P. Sartre, "L'existentialisme est un Humanisme," trans. Manet, in

W. Kaufmann (ed.), *Existentialism from Dostoevsky to Sartre* (New York, 1956), p. 295.

28. B. *Berachot* 33b.

29. A. N. Whitehead, *Process and Reality* (New York, 1929), p. 520.

30. L. Ford, "Divine Persuasion and the Triumph of the Good," in *Process Philosophy and Christian Thought*, ed. Brown and James (New York, 1971), p. 289.

31. Ibid., p. 290.

32. Whitehead, op. cit., p. 525.

33. Heschel, op. cit., p. 235.

34. Jeremiah 18:7–8.

35. Heschel, op. cit., pp. 218–219.

36. P. Tillich, *Love, Power, and Justice* (New York, 1954), pp. 70 ff.

37. W. Lippmann, *Preface to Morals* (New York, 1929), p. 111.

38. Isaiah 2:1–6.

39. W. Kaufmann, *The Faith of a Heretic* (New York, 1961), p. 217.

40. Micah 6:8.

41. *U.S. Supreme Courts Reports*, 26L Ed. 2d., *Welsh* vs *U.S.*, June 15, 1970.

42. Isaiah 46:10.

43. Isaiah 6:8–13.

44. Jeremiah 13:23.

45. Isaiah 2:2–4.

46. *Pirke Avot* II.

47. Jeremiah 31:28–34.

48. W. Paley, *Natural Theology* (London, 1836), 2:201.

49. R. Eisley, *Darwin's Century* (New York, 1958), p. 198.

50. *Foundation of the Origin of the Species*, ed. Francis Darwin (Cambridge, 1909), p. 51.

51. Tenant, op. cit., 2:107.

52. Ibid., p. 109.

53. Ibid., p. 111.

54. P. Bertocci, *Empirical Argument for God* (Cambridge, Mass., 1938 and 1970), pp. 235–237.

55. A. N. Whitehead, *The Function of Reason* (Boston, 1929), p. 7.

56. Ibid., p. 8.

57. Ford, op. cit., p. 289.

58. P. Hamilton, *The Living God and the Modern World* (Philadelphia, 1967), pp. 166–167.

59. Ford, op. cit., pp. 290–291.

60. Ogden, op. cit., p. 37.

61. Quoted in S. P. Schilling, *God in an Age of Atheism* (Nashville, 1969), pp. 164 ff.

62. S. Ogden, "Faith and Secularity," in *God and Secularization*, ed. L. E. F. Long (University of South Carolina Press, 1974), pp. 42–43.

CHAPTER 5

1. J. Barr, *Semantics of Biblical Language* (Oxford, 1961), p. 9.

2. Ibid., p. 13

3. F. Herzog, *Liberation Theology* (New York, 1972), p. 2.

4. Richard Niebuhr, *The Meaning of Revelation* (New York, 1941), p. 35.

5. J. H. Cone, *God of the Oppressed* (New York, 1975), p. 39.

6. V. A. Harvey, "What Is the Task of Theology," *Christianity and Crisis* 36 (May 24, 1976): 119.

7. G. Gutierrez, "Liberation Theology and Proclamation," in *Mystical and Political Dimension of Christian Faith* (New York, 1974), p. 69.

8. M. Daly, *Beyond God and Father* (Boston, 1973), p. 2

9. *New Yorker*, July 19, 1976, p. 68.

10. Ibid., p. 53.

11. R. Ruether, "What Is the Task of Theology" *Christianity and Crisis* 36 (May 24, 1976): 124.

12. Romans 3:28.

13. James 2:26.

14. Isaiah 31:1.

15. S. Blank, *Prophetic Faith in Isaiah* (New York, 1958), p. 35.

16. Hosea 2:21–22.

17. Habakkuk 2:4.

18. Isaiah 7:9.

19. Genesis 1:1–2.

20. Isaiah 48:6–7.

21. H. Cohen, *Judische Schriften*, pp. 402–404.

22. *Union Prayer Book*, newly revised ed., (1945), p. 256.

23. Psalm 90:17.

24. Hosea 14:2.

25. K. Kohler, *Jewish Theology* (New York, 1923), p. 241.

26. Amos 4:1, 4.

27. James 5:1–6 (New English Bible, 1961, p. 395).

28. E. Bloch, "Man as Responsibility," *Cross Currents* 18 (Summer 1968): 274.

29. G. Gutierrez, *Theology of Liberation* (New York, 1973), p. 32.

30. M. Daly, *Beyond the Father* (Boston, 1973), pp. 9–10.

31. C. Burch, "Creation, Technology, and Human Survival," *Ecumenical Review* 28 (1978): 70.

32. *Encyclopaedia Britannica*, 1970, s.v. "Capitalism," vol. 4, p. 842.

33. Jeremiah 22:13–16.

34. Jeremiah 34:17–18.

35. Isaiah 5:8.

36. Leviticus 25:10, 23, 24.

37. M. Buber, *Eclipse of God* (New York: Harpers Torchbooks, 1957), p. 7.

38. B. Russell, *A History of Western Philosophy* (New York, 1945), pp. 788 ff.

39. Isaiah 44:15–17.

40. N. Young, *Creator, Creation and Faith* (Philadelphia, 1976), p. 190.

41. P. Tillich, "The Attack of Dialectical Materialism on Christianity," *Student World* 31 (1938): 119.

42. *Reinhold Niebuhr on Politics*, ed. Davis and Good (New York, 1960), pp. 26–36.

43. G. Girardi, *Marxism and Christianity* (New York, 1968), p. 104.

44. C. Dickens, *A Tale of Two Cities* (London, 1850), bk. I, chap. 1.

45. R. Falk, *This Endangered Planet* (1971), pp. 42 ff.

46. R. Bellman.

47. K. Vonnegut.

48. Burch, op. cit., p. 73.

49. R. Heilbroner, *An Inquiry into the Human Prospect* (New York, 1974), pp. 47 ff.

50. C. Ayres, *Science the False Messiah* (Indianapolis, 1927).

51. M. Steinberg, *A Believing Jew* (New York, 1951), p. 37.

52. Ibid., p. 38 ff.

53. T. S. Eliot.

54. R. Heilbroner.

55. H. Jonas, "Technology and Responsibility," in *Philosophical Essays*, (Englewood, N.J., 1971), pp. 19–20.

56. P. Tillich, "The Attack of Dialectical Materialism on Christianity," *Student World* 31 (1938).

57. Deuteronomy 6:5–6.

58. Amos 5:1–2.

59. Amos 5:4–6.

60. Amos 9:14–15.